LawExpress
CRIMINOLOGY

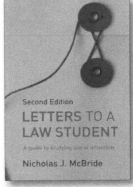

LawExpress

CRIMINOLOGY

Noel Cross
Liverpool John Moores University

PEARSON

Harlow, England • London • New York • Boston • San Francisco • Toronto • Sydney • Auckland • Singapore • Hong Kong
Tokyo • Seoul • Taipei • New Delhi • Cape Town • São Paulo • Mexico City • Madrid • Amsterdam • Munich • Paris • Milan

Pearson Education Limited
Edinburgh Gate
Harlow
Essex CM20 2JE
England

and Associated Companies throughout the world

Visit us on the World Wide Web at:
www.pearson.com/uk

First published 2013

© Pearson Education Limited 2013

ISBN 978-1-4058-7427-4

British Library Cataloguing-in-Publication Data
A catalogue record for this book is available from the British Library

Library of Congress Cataloging-in-Publication Data
A catalog record for this book is available from the Library of Congress

10 9 8 7 6 5 4 3
20 19 18 17

Typeset in 10/12pt HelveticaNeueLTPro by 71
Printed and bound by Ashford Colour Press Ltd, Gosport

Contents

Supporting resources

Visit the *Law Express* Series companion website at
www.pearsoned.co.uk/lawexpress to find valuable student learning material.

- A study plan test to help you assess how well you know the subject before you begin your revision
- Interactive quizzes to test your knowledge of the main points from each chapter
- Sample examination questions and guidelines for answering them
- Interactive flashcards to help you revise key theories and theorists, sources and terminology
- Printable versions of the topic maps and checklists from the book
- 'You be the marker' allows you to see exam questions and answers from the perspective of the examiner and includes notes on how an answer might be marked
- Podcasts provide point-by-point instruction on how to answer a common exam question

Also: The Companion Website provides the following features:

- Search tool to help locate specific items of content
- E-mail results and profile tools to send results of quizzes to instructors
- Online help and support to assist with website usage and troubleshooting

For more information please contact your local Pearson Education sales representative or visit **www.pearsoned.co.uk/lawexpress**

Acknowledgements

My thanks go to my wife, Helen, for her love and support during the time in which this book was prepared and written. My thanks also go to my colleagues in the School of Law at Liverpool John Moores University for their support and encouragement.

Noel Cross

Publisher's acknowledgements

Our thanks go to all reviewers who contributed to the development of this text, including students who participated in research and focus groups which helped to shape the series format.

Introduction

Criminology is the study of crime and criminal behaviour. Recently, it has become an increasingly common component on law programmes as well as being as an undergraduate programme subject in its own right. Criminal law is one of the core subjects required for a qualifying law degree, and criminology is a vital topic in relation to understanding the criminal law, because criminology studies a series of key analytical questions about the nature of crime: what it is, how much of it there is, who commits it, why they commit it, and how people who commit it should be punished. As such, criminology places the criminal law in the context of the society in which it operates, and provides a deeper understanding of why the criminal law is as it is, and of the reasons why the criminal law does not always operate effectively.

Because crime is such a fundamental feature of everyday life, especially in the mass media, most students who are studying criminology for the first time will have some ideas and preconceptions about how crime is defined, how much there is of it, what causes it and what should be done to stop it. It is essential that you do not allow these preconceptions about crime to influence your study and understanding of criminology as an academic area of study – not least because, as Chapter 4 in this book shows, media images of crime and its causes can be partial and misleading. Instead, you need to read as much reliable criminological literature as you can, and you also need to stay open-minded about the fact that there are many competing explanations for crime and its causes, all of which need to be considered and understood (if not necessarily agreed with) as you move through the different study areas which make up the field of criminology. You also need to remember that, despite what the media and politicians often claim, no one knows much about why crime occurs or what causes it!

This revision guide will help you to understand the key debates about what crime is, what causes crime, and how society can punish people who have committed crime. The guide is designed as a supplement to the lecture notes, course materials and books which you should already have as part of your criminology module or course – not as a replacement for those materials. As such, it should not be used as a short-cut around the detailed reading and thinking which you will need to do in order to understand criminology thoroughly. In fact, if used in the right way, this guide should do the opposite. It should encourage you to read more and think more deeply about the key issues and debates within the complex and contested field of criminology, firstly by ensuring that you understand the key issues and facts on a basic level, and secondly by showing how you can demonstrate a deeper level of understanding and reading, using the suggestions provided in each chapter to 'Make your answer stand out'. This guide does not provide a deep level of understanding for you, and cannot guarantee essay and exam success in criminology by itself. What it does aim to do is to guide you through the key issues which you need to understand for revision, and to offer advice on how you can organise and enhance your revision so as to maximise your chances of obtaining success through your own study and understanding.

📖 REVISION NOTE

- Don't be misled by public and media images of crime and its causes: approach each study topic in an academic way.

- Rely on this book as a guide to the process of revision – don't rely on it to tell you everything you need to know about criminology for essay and/or exam purposes.

- Focus on what your own course includes in terms of criminological content – lecture materials, handouts and recommended textbooks will act as a guide to which topic areas you need to focus on for revision, and give you a greater depth of knowledge and understanding if you use them properly.

- Get as much formative feedback as you can as you progress through your criminology course – feedback is essential for showing which areas you already understand, and which areas you need to work on, read around and revise in more depth.

- Be aware of the many connections and relationships between different criminological topic areas – essay and exam questions may cover more than one specific topic, so use the Revision notes in this book to help you to revise a topic area comprehensively by understanding how it relates to other topics.

Before you begin, you can use the study plan available on the companion website to assess how well you know the material in this book and identify the areas where you may want to focus your revision.

Guided tour

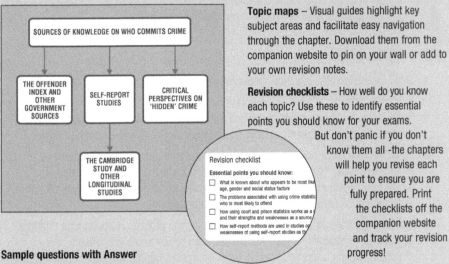

Topic maps – Visual guides highlight key subject areas and facilitate easy navigation through the chapter. Download them from the companion website to pin on your wall or add to your own revision notes.

Revision checklists – How well do you know each topic? Use these to identify essential points you should know for your exams. But don't panic if you don't know them all -the chapters will help you revise each point to ensure you are fully prepared. Print the checklists off the companion website and track your revision progress!

Sample questions with Answer guidelines – Practice makes perfect! Read the question at the start of each chapter and consider how you would answer it. Guidance on structuring strong answers is provided at the end of the chapter. Try out additional sample questions online.

> ### ▇ Sample question
>
> Could you answer this question? Below is a typical essay question that could arise on this topic. Guidelines on answering the question are included at the end of this chapter. Another sample question and guidance on tackling it can be found on the companion website.

Assessment advice – Not sure how best to tackle a question on a particular topic? Wondering what you may be asked? Use the assessment advice to identify the ways in which a subject may be examined and how to apply your knowledge effectively.

> ### ASSESSMENT ADVICE
>
> Essay and exam questions on who commits crime are likely to focus primarily on how reliable the difference measures of identifying offenders are, and what is (and can be) known and not known about who commits crime in England and Wales. Assessment questions are also likely to ask you which social factors – age, gender and so on – are most important in identifying who is most likely to commit crime, in terms of which factors appear to have the most influence over criminal behaviour.

Key definitions – Make sure you understand essential terminology. Use the flashcards online to test your recall!

> **KEY DEFINITION: Crime statistics**
>
> A range of ways of measuring crime, which give information about how many offences there are in a particular place and over a particular period of time, trends in the number of particular criminal offences or in crime generally over time, how many people are the victims of crime and how often they are victimised, and/or how often crime occurs in a particular area or to a particular social group.

Key theories, theorists and sources –
Identify and review the important elements
of the key theories
you will need to know for
your exam and the
theorists and sources
behind them.

KEY THEORY

The 'newsworthiness' of crim

Just as crime does not be
power to do so, so social
Writers such as Steve Chi
look for when selecting e

KEY THEORIST

David Farrington and the Cambridge Study in Delinquency

David Farrington and his colleagues at Cambridge University have provided the most
detailed and comprehensive attempt to overcome the criticisms of both official statistics
on offenders and smaller-scale self-report studies in the form of the Cambridge Study

KEY SOURCE

The Offenders Index

The Offenders Index is the most long-established method of identifying who is most
likely to commit crime in England and Wales. The Index is a record of who has been
convicted of an offence in court, and what that offence was. This information is currently

Make your answer stand out – This feature
illustrates sources of further thinking and
debate where you can maximise your marks.
Use them to really impress your examiners!

✓   Make your answer stand out

Read Steven Box (1981) for an extended critique of the methodology of self-report
studies, which includes more detailed arguments based around each of the points
identified above – but don't forget to question whether this source assumes too much

Exam tips – Feeling the pressure? These
boxes indicate how you can improve your
exam performance when it really counts.

EXAM TIP

Use different aspects of official government statistics on offenders to build up a more
complete picture of who commits crime. For example, a recently developed database
which offers much more detailed information than the Offender Index is the Offender

Revision notes – Get guidance for effective
revision. These boxes highlight related
points and areas of overlap in the subject,
or areas where your course might adopt a
particular approach that you should check
with your course tutor.

REVISION NOTE

Refer back to the discussion of the British Crime Survey and how much crime it reveals
is not reported or recorded in Chapter 2 to remind you of the limitations and social
construction of official statistics on offenders and offences. Also, refer back to the

Don't be tempted to . . . – This feature
underlines areas where students most often
trip up in exams. Use them to spot common
pitfalls and avoid losing marks.

!   Don't be tempted to . . .

Avoid making sweeping statements to the effect that the Offender Index can give a
complete picture of who commits crime in England and Wales. Evidence from other
sources on crime, such as the British Crime Survey, indicates that as much as 97

Be critical – Struggling with that vital
critical analysis? This feature will help you
identify contested areas and develop your
own arguments.

Be critical

Give your critical analysis of the Cambridge Study's methodology added depth by citing
criminologists such as Jock Young. Young has criticised the Study for overemphasising
individual and psychological factors, which could be apparent at a very young age, over

Read to impress – Focus on these
carefully selected sources to extend your
knowledge, deepen your understanding,
and earn better marks in coursework as
well as in exams.

READ TO IMPRESS

Becker, H. (1963) *Outsiders*, London: Macmillan.

Christie, N. (2004) *A Suitable Amount of Crime*, London: Routledge.

Hillyard, P. and Tombs, S. (2007), 'From "Crime" to "Social Harm"?', *Crime, Law and Social Change*,
48(1–2): 9–25.

Glossary – Forgotten the meaning of a
word? This quick reference covers key
definitions and other useful terms.

Glossary of terms

Guided tour of the companion website

 Book resources are available to download. Print your own **topic maps** and **revision checklists!**

 Use the **study plan** prior to your revision to help you assess how well you know the subject and determine which areas need most attention. Choose to take the full assessment or focus on targeted study units.

 'Test your knowledge' of individual areas with quizzes tailored specifically to each chapter. **Sample questions** are also available with guidance on crafting a good answer.

 Flashcards help improve recall of key theories and theorists, sources and terminology. Available in both electronic and printable formats.

'You be the marker' gives you the chance to evaluate sample exam answers and understand how and why an examiner awards marks.

Download the **podcast** and listen as your own personal Law Express tutor guides you through a 10–15 minute audio session. You will be presented with a typical but challenging question and provided a step-by-step explanation on how to approach the question, what essential elements your answer will need for a pass, how to structure a good response, and what to do to make your answer stand out so that you can earn extra marks.

All of this and more can be found when you visit
www.pearsoned.co.uk/lawexpress

What is crime?

1

Revision checklist

Essential points you should know:

- ☐ The key elements of what crime is
- ☐ The basic definition of crime as being against the law, and this approach's strengths and weaknesses
- ☐ The definition and meaning of crime as a social construct, and this approach's strengths and weaknesses
- ☐ Why and how what 'crime' is varies according to different places and different times
- ☐ The links between crime and social harm

■ Topic map

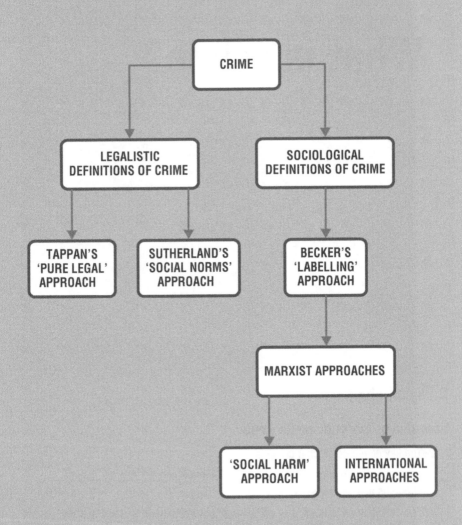

■ Introduction

Understanding crime is essential to understanding criminology.

If crime did not exist, there would be no need to have a criminal justice system to punish those who committed crime, and no need to understand the causes of crime. Yet crime, and its meaning, is often taken for granted or misunderstood in everyday life. This chapter aims to enable you to discuss the meaning of crime critically and accurately in an exam situation, and to understand how the meaning of crime has been approached in a variety of different ways by academic writers. In addition, the chapter also introduces later chapters on the causes of crime – because our understanding of what 'crime' is influences what we see as being the causes of criminal behaviour.

On the most basic level, crime is quite simply any behaviour which the criminal law says is illegal. Because this legal definition relies on what the criminal law says, there are some other characteristics of crime, taken from basic principles of the criminal law, which need to be added to the basic definition of crime above. These are:

- that the crime must be clearly defined as illegal when it is committed by someone;
- that the offender must have acted voluntarily (known as the *actus reus*, or guilty act);
- that the offender must have had some kind of blameworthy mental attitude at the time of committing the crime (known as the *mens rea*, or guilty mind);
- that none of the defences which are available in the criminal law apply to what the offender has done; and
- that there is a clearly defined punishment for committing the crime, which has been given to the offender.

ASSESSMENT ADVICE

The basic five-point definition of crime given above would be an accurate answer to the question of what crime is – but it would not get you many marks in a criminology exam! Essay and exam questions on what crime is will normally require you to show understanding of the different perspectives on what is, and what should be, included within the definition of 'crime'. You will need to recognise that 'crime' is a contested concept for criminologists, and be aware of the strengths and weaknesses of the various key approaches to understanding this issue.

■ Sample question

Could you answer this question? Below is a typical essay question that could arise on this topic. Guidelines on answering the question are included at the end of this chapter. Another sample question and guidance on tackling it can be found on the companion website.

ESSAY QUESTION

Critically discuss the idea that crime is best defined as any behaviour which is prohibited by the criminal law.

◼ Key theorists and theories in the definition of crime

KEY DEFINITION: Crime

Behaviour which is prohibited by the criminal law and which can be punished by the criminal justice system.

KEY THEORIST

Tappan and the pure legal approach

Tappan was a supporter of the basic legal definition of crime which is explained above. He argued that, because crime covers such a wide range of types of behaviour, the only meaningful way of defining it is to refer to what the criminal law defines as being a crime. Tappan therefore defined crime as an intentional act committed in violation of the criminal law, committed without defence or excuse, and punished by the state as a crime. He supported the definition of crime using the criminal law because, in his view, no other set of rules defines crime as clearly, precisely or objectively as the criminal law does.

Be critical

Focus on the vagueness in Tappan's definition in essay and exam answers. Think about whether, in your view, it is right to assume that we know about all the crime that is committed, in terms of recording and responding to it. Do you agree that the definition is right to assume that what the criminal law defines as being 'crime' never changes according to time and place?

Tappan's work can be criticised by looking at how the criminal law has developed in practice. For example, between 1997 and 2006, the New Labour Government created over 3,000 new criminal offences in England and Wales. On the other hand, some forms of behaviour used to be crimes but no longer are, such as homosexual behaviour between adult men (which was legalised in England and Wales by the Sexual Offences Act 1967). Also, some forms of behaviour are not crimes in England and Wales, but are crimes in other countries – such as adultery, which is a crime in some Muslim countries, such as Pakistan and Saudi Arabia.

Thirdly, the legal definition does not tell us anything about why some kinds of behaviour are made criminal, but other kinds are not (or about how criminal justice enforces the law in practice). To answer these questions, we need to look beyond the basic legal definition of crime and examine other key writers' perspectives on what crime is, and what it should be.

KEY THEORIST

Sutherland and law as social and moral norms

Sutherland was critical of Tappan's limitation of the definition of crime to criminal acts punished by the courts. Instead, he argued that we need to define crime as being types of behaviour which are objectively seen as being morally wrong and harmful to society in general. It is these **socially harmful acts**, Sutherland stated, which the state defines and punishes as crimes. The idea of crime reflecting morality can be related to historic writings stating that law reflected (or should reflect) the teachings of various religions.

Be critical

You should criticise Sutherland's definition for assuming that crime can be defined according to the objective criteria of morally wrong and socially harmful acts. If this was true, the criminal law would always stay the same in terms of what it defined as crime. As we saw above when discussing Tappan's work, the criminal law regularly changes shape over time, and from state to state. You should also discuss Sutherland's assumption that society as a whole always agrees about which acts are morally and socially harmful (and therefore deserve to be punished as crimes), and which are not.

Evidence from public opinion polls suggests that there is no consensus on whether some crimes should actually be crimes. For example, possession of cannabis involves committing the offence of possessing a Class B drug, which is punishable by a maximum sentence of five years' imprisonment in England and Wales. Yet various public opinion polls have estimated that 50 – 60 percent of young adults think that possession of cannabis should not be a crime. This suggests that Sutherland is wrong about there being a complete consensus in society about what crime should be.

1 WHAT IS CRIME?

KEY THEORIST

Becker and crime as 'labelling'

Becker rejected the idea that there is a consensus in society about what is and should be seen as crime, and that the criminal law represents this consensus. Instead, he saw crime as the result of certain individuals' and groups' perceptions of deviant behaviour. On this view, some types of behaviour are labelled as being criminal by certain individuals or groups in society. Various criminal justice agencies whose job it is to implement and enforce the criminal law (e.g. police, lawyers, the courts and government officials who shape criminal law and criminal justice policy) engage in a series of negotiations which may or may not result in behaviour being defined as a crime, depending on how successfully the criminal 'label' can be applied.

On Becker's view, criminal law can and does change according to time and place. Similarly, what counts as crime also changes according to who can successfully pin the criminal label on whom in society at any given time, and how particular 'deviant' individuals and groups are selected for criminalisation and punishment. In order to understand what crime is, we need to understand the processes of how criminal law is created, defined and used in practice by criminal justice agencies. According to Becker, we also need to understand that crime is a **social construct**, shaped and defined by those who have the power to make and enforce the law.

📖 REVISION NOTE

When revising this topic, read the material on labelling theory in Chapter 8 below as well, to enhance your understanding of Becker's ideas on the definition and causes of crime.

Be critical

When discussing Becker's labelling theory in an essay or exam, emphasise not only its advantages (such as that it can explain why the content of criminal law changes frequently according to time and place, in terms of laws being 'socially constructed' and negotiated between individuals and groups in society which have the power to label – e.g. those who make criminal law and other powerful groups such as the media) but also its disadvantages, such as its failure to clearly explain *why* 'labelling' takes place.

KEY THEORY

The Marxist approaches to defining crime

A Marxist approach was applied to the definition of crime from the late 1960s onwards. Becker's labelling theory was a key influence on these Marxist approaches. Writers such as William Chambliss and Richard Quinney focused on the ability of the powerful in society to control the powerless, and protect their own social and economic interests, through their ability to define what 'crime' is and shape the criminal law. These powerful sections of society can also use their power to define and enforce the criminal law to focus society's attention on the types of crime usually committed by the powerless through the ability to 'morally censure' (as Colin Sumner argued) those who are seen as a threat to the social and economic interests of the powerful. Those in a position of power can then divert attention away from their own more socially harmful wrongdoing in a process which the criminologist Steven Box termed 'mystification'.

✎ EXAM TIP

When discussing Marxist approaches to defining crime, make sure that you emphasise Becker's influence on these approaches. Becker's argument, that crime definition was centrally concerned with who has the ability to label whom as criminal, was a vital foundation of Marxist thoughts on crime definition.

Be critical

You could criticise pure Marxist approaches like these for placing too much blame on capitalism as a cause of the exploitation of the powerless by the powerful through criminal law. Analyse this claim on a deeper level by discussing writers who, while still broadly supportive of the Marxist approach, have criticised pure Marxists for overstating the ability of the powerful to control the rest of society through criminal law.

▶

E.P. Thompson, for example, argued in his work on the historical development of the criminal law that, although criminal law was expanded in the past to protect ruling-class interests (e.g. by criminalising the previous legal activity of poaching animals from someone else's land), the working class played an active role in changes to the criminal law, and these changes were the result of class struggle and protest as well as changes in politics and the economy.

The Marxist approach to the 'social construction' of crime is still influential today. Nils Christie, for example, has argued that 'crime' does not exist at all. Instead, there are only acts which are given negative social meanings under certain social conditions – in other words, which are defined as criminal in a particular place and time – and, on Christie's view, criminologists can only study the conditions which lead to acts being defined as criminal in this way. Christie also argues that the powerful in society use their power to make sure that there is always enough crime in a society to suit their interests – by allowing them to make a profit from privatising prisons which detain convicted offenders, for example.

 Make your answer stand out

A key debate on labelling theory relates to the extent of its influence on the Marxist approach to the definition of crime discussed below. Contrast the arguments of Becker (1963) with the work of Christie (2004), who denies that there is any objective basis to the measurement of crime while arguing that the state attempts to define the nature and extent of crime to enhance its own power and ability to socially control the public, so as to assess the influence of labelling theory on later approaches.

KEY THEORY

The post-Marxist 'social harm' approach to crime definition

Another recent offshoot from the Marxist approach is the 'social harm' movement, developed by Paddy Hillyard, Steve Tombs and others. This approach argues that criminologists should stop focusing on how 'crime' is officially defined and concentrate instead on all activities which can be seen as socially harmful – not only criminal behaviour itself, but also poor healthcare, poor education and social inequality – so as to find the causes of these problems. On this view, crime is not a special category of behaviour at all. It is rather one of a range of social problems, all of which should be addressed and punished.

Be critical

You could criticise the 'social harm' standpoint for its contradictory approach to defining crime. On the one hand, its supporters criticise the powerful for exploiting the rest of society through unjust criminal law; but on the other, they argue for broadening the scope of criminal law to cover other types of social harm as well as crime itself, which might lead to a further increase in the use of criminal law to increase social control and repression in society, as Richard Ericson has pointed out.

! Don't be tempted to . . .

Avoid discussing all of the Marxist-influenced approaches to defining crime in the same way in an essay or exam question. The more recent approaches, such as the 'social harm' approach, lose the earlier focus on crime as a particular type of social behaviour, instead seeing crime as just one type of socially harmful activity. Similarly, traditional Marxists give the powerful a far greater ability to control the powerless through changing the criminal law than E.P. Thompson's work does.

KEY THEORY

Globalised approaches to defining crime

Wayne Morrison argues that our definitions of crime are too focused on individual behaviour and on how individual nation states respond to crime through the criminal law. He claims that these definitions do not take social, economic and political globalisation into account. In other words, with the growth in behaviour which can be viewed as criminal but which involves people from more than one country – so-called international crime – it is no longer enough to rely on individual countries to define what 'crime' is and what the response to it should be. Instead, Morrison argues that we need a new set of universal, international definitions of criminal behaviour to define crime properly. In support of his argument, Morrison points to famous incidents of criminal behaviour from various points in history, such as the Holocaust during the second World War or the attacks on the Twin Towers in New York on 11 September 2001, which wrongly were either not defined or not responded to as 'crimes' by the international community.

Be critical

Bring critical analysis of Morrison's views into an essay or exam by arguing that it might be impossible to construct universal, internationally driven definitions of crime which can take into account all the types of criminal behaviour which occur in society, since criminal law covers such a wide range of offences.

> **✎ EXAM TIP**
>
> Expand your discussion of radical approaches to defining crime in an exam or essay by including analysis of Morrison's internationally focused arguments on definition. Morrison's view is influenced by critical thinking on the social construction of crime, but he takes a much wider view of the definition of crime than most Marxist writers do, because he focuses on crime which occurs on an international level, which allows serious forms of crime (e.g. genocide) to be considered as criminal behaviour.

■Putting it all together

Answer guidelines

See the essay question at the start of the chapter.

Approaching the question

This question is asking you about the best way to define what 'crime' is. You would therefore want to show your understanding of the range of ways in which key writers have argued we should define crime, explaining the strengths and weaknesses of each approach to add valuable critical analysis to your answer.

Important points to include

- Introduction indicating the general scope of the question and mapping out the overall structure of the essay in brief.
- Show awareness that the specific subject matter of the question relates to the purely legalistic approach to defining crime, as developed by Paul Tappan, and discuss weaknesses of this approach.
- Discussion of Edwin Sutherland's definition of crime as behaviour which is objectively seen as morally and socially harmful by society, and critical consideration of Sutherland's work's strengths and weaknesses.
- Discussion of Howard Becker's 'labelling' approach to defining crime, and critical consideration of its strengths and weaknesses.
- Discussion of the range of approaches to defining crime which could be described as Marxist, with critical consideration of the different Marxist approaches' strengths and weaknesses.
- Discussion of the international or globalised approach to defining crime shown in the work of Wayne Morrison, again with critical consideration of the strengths and weaknesses of this approach.

- Conclusion summarising the essay's arguments, assessing the relative merit of the different approaches to defining crime which have been put forward, and showing the level of agreement or disagreement with the claim made in the question's title.

 Make your answer stand out

- Emphasise the evolution of ideas about defining crime from the early approaches based on the definition of the criminal law, through to more recent ideas relating to crime as a social construction, locating its definition within events in wider society at any given time. Bringing a sense of the development of ideas over time, and a sense of the social and historical context in which key ideas were developed, into your answer will provide a more effective structure, as well as making it easier for you to analyse each set of ideas critically.

- Emphasise common themes shared between different approaches as well as differences, to make it easier to show the strengths and weaknesses of each in defining what 'crime' is effectively. For example, the Marxist approaches share a focus on the inequality of social power and the ability of the powerful (who can affect the criminal law) to use criminal law to protect their own interests – but a writer such as E.P. Thompson argues that lower-class people can have an influence on how the criminal law develops, whereas such writers as William Chambliss focus far more on the ability of the powerful to manipulate the powerless through the definition of the criminal law.

- Include as wide a range of writers' ideas as you can, to show a deep understanding of the diversity of approaches to defining crime.

READ TO IMPRESS

Becker, H. (1963) *Outsiders*, London: Macmillan.

Christie, N. (2004) *A Suitable Amount of Crime*, London: Routledge.

Hillyard, P. and Tombs, S. (2007), 'From "Crime" to "Social Harm"?', *Crime, Law and Social Change*, **48**(1–2): 9–25.

Morrison, W. (2006) *Criminology, Civilisation and the New World Order*, London: Routledge.

Tappan, P.W. (1947), 'Who is the Criminal?', *American Sociological Review*, **12**: 96–102.

www.pearsoned.co.uk/lawexpress

Go online to access more revision support, including quizzes to test your knowledge, sample questions with answer guidelines, podcasts you can download, and more!

Measuring crime

2

■ Topic map

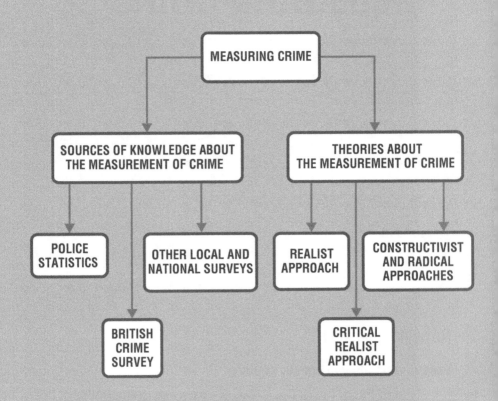

■ Introduction

Crime is an extremely popular and controversial topic in today's society.

Politicians, the media and the public spend a lot of time debating whether crime has gone up or down recently, and what trends can be seen for particular offences in different parts of England and Wales. However, crime statistics come in more than one format – there are a range of things which each format cannot tell us about how much crime there is, as well as a range of things which each one can provide information on. In fact, radical criminologists such as Steven Box and Nils Christie have argued that crime statistics tell us as much about the people who compile them – in terms of their values and interests – and the attitudes of society towards crime as about the nature and extent of crime itself. This chapter will give you guidance on assessing how much is known and not known about crime in England and Wales, as well as on evaluating the relative strengths and weaknesses of the different ways of measuring crime.

ASSESSMENT ADVICE

Essay and exam questions on the measurement of crime will normally go beyond a straightforward discussion of how much crime there is currently. Instead, the focus is likely to be on the strengths and weaknesses of particular ways of measuring crime, or on the extent to which different types of crime are knowable or unknowable through the crime statistics which are available. When attempting a question like this, always bear in mind the ways in which crime statistics are 'socially constructed' by certain social groups, the different ways in which crime statistics are used by different social groups, and the effects that social construction has on what we know and don't know about crime.

■ Sample question

Could you answer this question? Below is a typical essay question that could arise on this topic. Guidelines on answering the question are included at the end of this chapter. Another sample question and guidance on tackling it can be found on the companion website.

ESSAY QUESTION

'Given the nature of the "dark figure" of crime, the true extent of crime in England and Wales is unknowable.' Critically discuss this statement.

■ Key sources, theories and theorists in measuring crime

KEY DEFINITION: Crime statistics

A range of ways of measuring crime, which give information about how many offences there are in a particular place and over a particular period of time, trends in the number of particular criminal offences or in crime generally over time, how many people are the victims of crime and how often they are victimised, and/or how often crime occurs in a particular area or to a particular social group.

□ REVISION NOTE

When thinking about and revising the social construction of crime statistics, read the discussion of the social construction of crime itself in Chapter 1 to remind you of the processes by which social construction works.

It is vital to understand that there are a range of sources of statistics on crime, each with its own way of measuring crime, and each with its own strengths and weaknesses as a means of understanding how much crime there is in society.

KEY SOURCE

Police-recorded crime statistics

The crimes which are recorded by the police in England and Wales, as a result of reports from the public, police work or confessions from arrested offenders, form the basis of one of the main types of crime statistics.

Crimes recorded by police are known as **notifiable offences** and are divided into ten categories: violence against the person, sexual offences, robbery, burglary, theft, handling stolen goods, fraud and forgery, criminal damage, drugs offences and 'other offences', a category which covers any offence that does not fit into any of the other categories. Police statistics are published quarterly by the government, as well as in an annual report which combines them with data from the British Crime Survey (see below).

Be critical

Use Maguire (2007) to point out the limitations of police statistics in terms of understanding how much crime there really is in England and Wales. You could argue, firstly, that the criminal law itself can and does change over time – behaviour is criminalised or decriminalised, and this affects the types of behaviour which are recorded by the police as crimes.

Formal government rules on crime recording can also change the shape of crime data. For example, in 1998, some offences which were previously summary offences, and therefore not counted in the police criminal statistics (such as common assault), started to be counted as notifiable – an important influence on subsequent apparent increases in the amount of violent crime in the police statistics.

The police still have a great deal of discretion over whether or not to record offences which are reported to them by the public, despite the introduction of National Crime Recording Standards nationally in 2002. There are a range of reasons why the police might not record crime which is reported to them (the 'grey figure' of crime), as Bottomley and Pease (1986) note, such as:

- a low chance of the offender being prosecuted and convicted; or

- pressure on police to prove their effectiveness in detecting and reducing crime, which might result in the non-recording of some offences to improve the 'clear up' rate of offender detection.

Lastly, the police can only record what the public report, and public reporting behaviour can and does change over time as public attitudes towards different crimes and towards the police vary. Public fear of a particular type of crime, for example, can increase reporting rates, and therefore increase recording rates by the police.

KEY DEFINITION: The 'dark figure' of crime

Crime which is not reported to the police by the public, and which therefore cannot be included in police recorded crime statistics.

✎ EXAM TIP

When critically analysing the usefulness of police crime statistics, relate the limitations of these statistics to wider developments in society and politics to obtain extra marks. Societal changes such as the decline in public trust in the police can be used to explain how police crime statistics are compiled, and why they give a limited picture of crime overall.

The British Crime Survey

The **British Crime Survey** (BCS) asks a sample of the population of England and Wales about their experiences as victims of crime, as well as related issues, such as whether or not they reported their crime to the police. Currently the BCS surveys over 45,000 people in England and Wales every year, although it has only included people under the age of 16 in the survey since 2009.

It asks whether participants have been a victim of crime in the previous year and, if they have, what type of crime it was who the offender was and other information related to the offence. The major advantage of the BCS compared with police crime statistics is that it can, and does, record some crime which was not reported to the police by the victim – in other words, it can uncover some of the 'dark figure' of crime.

Be critical

You need to be aware of the limitations of BCS data as well as the limitations of police statistics – don't fall into the trap of assuming that, because the BCS can capture some crime which is unreported to the police, it is a flawless data source. You should think about and discuss, firstly, the issue of the BCS only asking a sample of the entire population about crime, so that most of the population of England and Wales are not included in the survey, even though the BCS sample is meant to be as close to the general population in terms of demographics as possible. You also need to think about the extent to which the BCS's other limitations damage its reliability. For example, it only includes private households, so anyone who does not have a postcode (e.g. a homeless person) will not be included in the survey, and neither is crime which is committed against businesses.

The BCS also only counts a maximum of six incidents per participant, so 'extra' crime which a victim reports might not be recorded for this reason. Another problem is that the BCS relies on accurate public reporting of offences and there are a range of reasons why respondents might not give accurate information, such as:

- the victim is unaware of the fact that they are a victim (e.g. they have been the victim of fraud without realising);
- the victim has forgotten what happened to them;
- the victim is too afraid to tell the surveyor what happened (e.g. in cases of domestic violence where the victim and offender are still living in the same house); or
- the victim mistakenly believes an offence is within the time period when it actually happened over a year ago.

The BCS does not have a large enough sample or detailed enough data to measure crime on a local level, area by area. Lastly, the BCS cannot cover homicide, because the victims of this group of offences are dead and therefore cannot be questioned!

✎ EXAM TIP

When assessing whether the BCS is a useful source of knowledge on crime, show knowledge of the results of the first BCS surveys, including children under the age of 16, from 2009 onwards. Does the data on child victimisation rates which these surveys have produced add to the usefulness of crime knowledge generated by the BCS as a whole?

KEY SOURCE

Other local and national crime and victimisation surveys

Other sources of crime data have attempted to fill the gaps left behind by the police and BCS statistics. Firstly, various **local victimisation surveys** have been completed at various times in specific areas in England and Wales. Often these surveys have been carried out in inner city areas, to illustrate the fact that the risk of being the victim of crime can be considerably higher than the national victimisation average (as calculated by the BCS) for those who come from a deprived socio-economic background or who are part of a specific social group, such as ethnic minorities. Examples of this type of survey include the Islington Crime Surveys carried out in London in 1986 and 1989, which revealed far higher rates of crime (especially property crime) than the BCS had for the same area. These victim surveys have been crucial in raising political and public awareness of the experiences of different types of crime victim.

Some exploratory local surveys have focused on specific types of criminal offence, especially crimes which were traditionally rarely reported to either the police or the BCS, such as rape or domestic violence. Ruth Hall's survey on the extent of rape in London in the mid-1980s is an example of this type of source. The Commercial Victimisation Survey was carried out by the Home Office in 1994 and 2002 to gather information on crime committed against businesses, a type of crime not included in BCS data, and self-report studies such as the Offending Crime and Justice Survey have attempted to measure crime through asking survey respondents about their own criminal behaviour. Lastly, various attempts have been made to gather information on crimes which are committed in more than one country, such as transnational organised crime and people-trafficking (mostly data from government organisations such as the Serious Organised Crime Agency), and crimes against international law, such as state crimes or crimes during war (mostly data from human rights campaign groups such as Amnesty International).

Be critical

You need to discuss the limitations of these alternative sources in the same way as you would approach critical analysis of the mainstream crime data sources. None of these surveys are comprehensive, a point you would need to emphasise in critical analysis. The local crime surveys (such as Ruth Hall's London-based study) obviously only relate to one particular area rather than the whole of England and Wales as the police and BCS data claim to – so they cannot, for example, be used to compare crime rates in different areas. Also the specific crime type surveys only give details of particular types of crime, and so do not allow for the occurrence of different types of crime to be compared.

These surveys also do not use a standard method of collecting data as the BCS does, and differences in methods of collecting data can affect the answers given by participants – so these sources' results are not directly comparable to the data drawn from the police and the BCS. Also, the data obtained through these measures is not always reliable – in self-report studies, for example, respondents may fail to disclose crime which they have committed to avoid 'looking bad' or 'getting into trouble'. In relation to international and war crimes, the data is not gathered systematically, and sometimes information on incidents which are extremely harmful socially (e.g. genocide) is either not considered as 'crime' at all or not considered as a type of crime statistic.

 Make your answer stand out

Karstedt and Farrall's (2006) research questions the usefulness of crime statistics in terms of investigating how much crime (especially crime committed by middle- and upper-class people) is not picked up by any crime measures, and attempts to make theoretical sense of why this is the case. This source can also be used as support for arguments that the measurement of crime is in itself distorted by the powerful in society promoting their own interests and masking their own criminal behaviour.

KEY THEORY

The realist approach

This approach to measuring crime claims that crime statistics are an accurate indicator of the amount of crime in society at any one time, and of society's attitudes towards different types of crime.

Government publications of crime statistics – both police and BCS data – take the view that crime statistics are a reliable indicator of trends in different types of crime over time, and governments regularly use crime statistics as a justification for different criminal justice policies, considering information from police recording and the BCS side by side as the basis for policies.

KEY THEORY

The critical realist approach

Critical realism shares conventional realism's view that crime statistics should be taken seriously and can give a realistic picture of crime. However, critical realists question the universal applicability to crime and victimisation statistics to the entire population.

This view of measuring crime was the theoretical driving force behind the local crime surveys carried out in the 1980s in England and Wales, which highlighted the disproportionate risks of crime victimisation faced by those who were poor, from ethnic minorities or young people, and compared the risk of being victimised with rates of fear of crime. The approach was influenced heavily by the work of the criminologist Jock Young (1988). This theory can be seen as a 'middle way' between the conventional realist approach and the constructivist approach explained below – the critical realist approach accepts that some things (such as crime) are objectively measurable to a certain extent, but also claims that people subjectively interpret the concept of crime for themselves, and that this interpretation can affect perceptions of the seriousness of crime (and fear of crime) as well as the ways in which crime is measured.

 Make your answer stand out

Use the critique of the conventional realist position on crime measurement by Young (1988) to illustrate the strengths and weaknesses of the critical realist approach in an exam answer.

KEY THEORY

The constructivist and radical approaches

The constructivist approach to measuring crime criticises the realist approach for failing to consider the social context in which crime statistics are shaped and constructed. On this view, crime statistics cannot present an objective and accurate picture of crime. Instead, they only provide a partial snapshot of crime, subjectively filtered through the activities of the individuals and agencies who construct the crime statistics.

The constructivist view would argue, for example, that police statistics in England and Wales are affected by a whole range of factors which distort the picture of crime presented in those statistics – the use of crime statistics to measure the effectiveness of police performance by central government might mean that certain types of crime are under- or over-recorded, for example – and that, as a result, crime statistics tell us as much about the people who collect them as about crime itself. It is this approach which has developed the view that crime statistics are socially constructed by the police and other agencies.

Some radical writers, such as Steven Box (1981), have gone further than the constructivists, stating that crime statistics say nothing objective about crime, and in fact deliberately 'hide' the social processes which drive the measurement of crime, as well as purposely hiding socially harmful activity (e.g. corporate or state crime) committed by the powerful in society, which is not considered as being 'crime' for the purposes of crime measurement and statistics.

 Make your answer stand out

The constructivist approach to crime statistics developed largely from the work of Cicourel (1968), so critically discuss this source in your exam answer to show greater depth of understanding. Also, for a radical view on the manipulation of both crime and criminal statistics by the powerful to hide their own wrongdoing and to repress the socially 'troublesome' activities of the less powerful in society, read Box (1981) – again, question this source in terms of whether it in fact overestimates the ability of the state to impose its own interests on the rest of society through the definition and measurement of crime.

📖 REVISION NOTE

To enhance your understanding of the constructivist and radical approaches, revise this material together with the discussion of labelling theory criminology (which shares the constructivist approach) in Chapter 8, and with the discussion of Marxist criminology (which shares the radical approach) in Chapter 9.

■ Crime measurement's influences on criminal justice policy

As Tim Hope notes, individuals and groups in society use crime statistics as a source of information about the nature and extent of crime, locally, nationally or both, in a variety of ways. Governments regularly use statistics, and media coverage of statistics, as a basis and justification for their criminal justice policies, which are designed to respond to crime effectively. An example of this process can be seen in drugs classification policy in England and Wales – changing media coverage of incidents of cannabis usage influenced the Government to move the drug from class B to class C in 2004, and back to class B in 2009.

As a result, crime statistics, and their interpretation by the media, play a key role in developing criminal justice policy – sometimes at the expense of more detailed academic research on crime, and despite the limitations of both police records and the BCS in capturing crime. As well as central government, local councils and police forces also use crime statistics to assess their own performance, often in response to central government demands for evaluation of criminal justice effectiveness in detecting and preventing crime. Since the BCS cannot measure crime street by street, local agencies are forced to use police recorded crime statistics for this purpose, which again means that policies may be based on misleading information about the nature and extent of crime in a particular area.

The public also use crime statistics in a number of ways. Crime statistics which claim to show how much crime, and which types of crime, there are in a particular area are commonly accessed by the public. An example of public interest in how much crime there is in their area can be seen in the popularity of a police crime mapping website which showed the extent and nature of crime at individual street level. When it was launched in early 2011, this website was receiving an estimated 75,000 hits per minute.

The public also use crime statistics to analyse criminal justice agencies' effectiveness at a local and national level. However, the Statistics Commission Review (carried out by the government in 2006) suggested that the public rely heavily on the government, the media and academics to help them make sense of crime statistics. Often the public do not receive the help that they need in this respect – for example, when the media fail to explain why police crime statistics and BCS data show opposite trends in the occurrence of specific crimes or in the crime rate generally.

While the public's usage of crime statistics, therefore, can be very influential in the development of criminal justice policy, as local and national government try to win the public's vote in elections, the public's understanding of crime can be as misleading and partial as crime statistics themselves.

■Putting it all together

Answer guidelines

See the essay question at the start of the chapter.

Approaching the question

This question is asking you how much is known, and how much can be known, about the nature and extent of crime in England and Wales. This requires knowledge of how the major sources of knowledge about crime rates operate, and what their strengths and weaknesses are in practice.

▶

Important points to include

■ Introduction mapping out the overall structure of the essay in brief.

■ Identification of the key theoretical positions on crime measurement – the conventional realist, critical realist and constructivist approaches – and how much each one claims that crime statistics can tell us about crime.

■ Explanation of police crime statistics – how they are compiled and structured, their weaknesses in terms of not capturing crime (emphasising the 'dark figure' and 'grey figure' of crime).

■ Explanation of the British Crime Survey – how it is compiled and structured, its strengths in relation to the police statistics and the 'dark figure', and its weaknesses.

■ Explanation of alternative ways of measuring crime, such as victimisation surveys, with awareness of how each approach's strengths and weaknesses in terms of recording crime.

■ Conclusions summarising the essay's arguments and explaining the essay's position on the claim in the question.

 Make your answer stand out

■ Integrate theoretical perspectives on crime measurement into the essay, linking these perspectives into practical ways of measuring crime – for example, links could be made between the conventional realist approach and police crime statistics, and the ways in which those statistics are interpreted and taken at face value by the public, politicians and the media.

■ Use as much academic research on the effectiveness and accuracy of crime statistics as you can, to add extra critical analysis.

■ Use up-to-date knowledge of crime trends in England and Wales, particularly police and BCS data, from government websites to evidence wider reading – but make sure that you relate this knowledge clearly to the question, to avoid the discussion becoming too descriptive.

READ TO IMPRESS

Bottomley, A.K. and Pease, K. (1986) *Crime and Punishment: Interpreting the data,* Milton Keynes: Open University Press.

Box, S. (1981) *Deviance, Reality and Society* (2nd edn), London: Holt, Rinehart and Winston.

Cicourel, A. (1968) *The Social Organisation of Juvenile Justice,* New York: Wiley.

Karstedt, S. and Farrall, S. (2006) 'The Moral Economy of Everyday Crime: Markets, consumers and citizens', *British Journal of Criminology,* **46**(6): 1011–36.

Maguire, M. (2007) 'Crime Data and Statistics', in Maguire, M., Morgan, R. and Reiner, R. (eds) The Oxford Handbook of Criminology (4th edn), Oxford: Oxford University Press.

Young, J. (1988) 'Risk of Crime and Fear of Crime: A realist critique of survey-based assumptions', in Maguire, M. and Pointing, J. (eds.), *Victims of Crime: A new deal?,* Milton Keynes: Open University Press.

www.pearsoned.co.uk/lawexpress

 Go online to access more revision support, including quizzes to test your knowledge, sample questions with answer guidelines, podcasts you can download and more!

Who commits crime?

3

Revision checklist

Essential points you should know:

☐ What is known about who appears to be most likely to commit crime, in terms of age, gender and social status factors

☐ The problems associated with using crime statistics measures for information on who is most likely to offend

☐ How using court and prison statistics works as a measure of finding offenders, and their strengths and weaknesses as a source of information on offenders

☐ How self-report methods are used in studies on offenders, and the strengths and weaknesses of using self-report studies as the basis for information on offenders

■Topic map

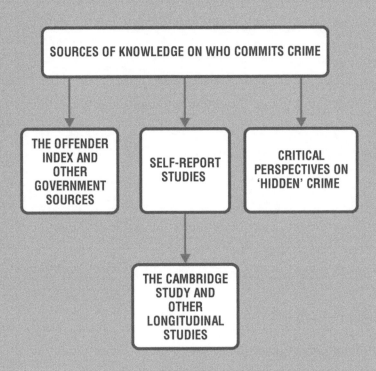

■ Introduction

Although Chapter 2 showed that a wide variety of information is now available about crime in England and Wales in terms of offences which are committed, both from police records and through data obtained from victims of crime in the British Crime Survey, there has been less focus on information about offenders.

This reflects the move away from focusing on the characteristics of individual offenders, and on the causes of crime, and towards focusing on crime prevention and punishment, in criminal justice policy – issues which will be discussed later on in this book. This chapter looks at what is known and not known about who is most likely to commit crime in England and Wales – an area of investigation which takes into account a range of social issues, such as age, gender, race and social class, which might influence the questions of who becomes an offender, and why.

ASSESSMENT ADVICE

Essay and exam questions on who commits crime are likely to focus primarily on how reliable the difference measures of identifying offenders are, and what is (and can be) known and not known about who commits crime in England and Wales. Assessment questions are also likely to ask you which social factors – age, gender and so on – are most important in identifying who is most likely to commit crime, in terms of which factors appear to have the most influence over criminal behaviour.

■ Sample question

Could you answer this question? Below is a typical essay question that could arise on this topic. Guidelines on answering the question are included at the end of this chapter. Another sample question and guidance on tackling it can be found on the companion website.

ESSAY QUESTION

Critically discuss the argument that age is the most important factor in determining who is most likely to commit crime in England and Wales.

Key sources, theorists and theories in measuring who commits crime

KEY SOURCE

The Offenders Index

The Offenders Index is the most long-established method of identifying who is most likely to commit crime in England and Wales. The Index is a record of who has been convicted of an offence in court, and what that offence was. This information is currently included in the publication *Criminal Statistics: England and Wales,* published quarterly by the Ministry of Justice. The Index also collects other information about offenders, such as their age, gender and ethnic background.

The Index is able to measure the demographics of offenders in several ways. For example, recent statistics show that in the 12 months to March 2011 in England and Wales:

- 76.7 percent of all those convicted by magistrates' or Crown Courts were male;
- 5.3 percent of all those convicted were 17 years old or under; and
- around 75 percent of all those convicted were White.

These data have the advantage of being accurately and systematically collected and analysed by the government. They can also measure demographic offender trends over time – for example, Home Office Research conducted in the 1990s revealed that, of males born in 1953, over a third had a criminal conviction before their 40th birthday, and they were most likely to have been convicted of theft or burglary, with violence against the person being the third most common conviction category.

✎ EXAM TIP

Use different aspects of official government statistics on offenders to build up a more complete picture of who commits crime. For example, a recently developed database which offers much more detailed information than the Offender Index is the Offender Assessment System (OASyS). OASyS was only set up in 2003, but it offers detailed information on an offender's social situation – for example, whether they use drugs, or how much education they have received – which the Offender Index does not cover. Prison statistics, such as those in a Social Exclusion Unit report on the demographics of prisoners published in 2002, also reveal that disproportionately high numbers of prisoners are unemployed, from an ethnic minority background, less than 30 years old, have spent time in care and are poorly educated compared with the general population.

Be critical

You need to emphasise what government offender statistics do not cover in relation to understanding who commits crime. You could do this, for example, by reflecting on the fact that most crime does not reach the conviction stage, and so the people who committed these crimes do not appear in the Offender Index, or in OASyS or prison statistics. In fact, any crime which has not been reported, not been recorded or not been successfully prosecuted will not feature in any of these statistics.

Other problems relate to the differences between the various measures of who commits crime. OASyS, for example, uses a standardised scale to measure the prevalence of social issues in a particular offender's life, going beyond the basic counting of convictions contained in the Offender Index. These differences make it difficult to compare the different sources of information on offenders directly and accurately.

! Don't be tempted to . . .

Avoid making sweeping statements to the effect that the Offender Index can give a complete picture of who commits crime in England and Wales. Evidence from other sources on crime, such as the British Crime Survey, indicates that as much as 97 percent of crime does not result in anyone being cautioned or convicted for it. It is impossible to tell who committed this 97 percent or what these offenders' demographics are from the information contained in the Offenders Index.

☐ REVISION NOTE

Refer back to the discussion of the British Crime Survey and how much crime it reveals is not reported or recorded in Chapter 2 to remind you of the limitations and social construction of official statistics on offenders and offences. Also, refer back to the discussion of crime itself as a social construct in [Chapter 1], and think about how the changing nature of crime could limit what we know about who commits crime.

KEY SOURCE

Self-report studies

Self-report studies are surveys in which a sample of the population in a country is asked, confidentially, how often they have committed crime over a certain period of time and which types of crime they have committed. In this way, self-report studies are ▶

able to build up a picture of who commits crime and have a key advantage over official statistics such as the Offenders Index in that they are able to avoid the problems of the non-reporting, non-recording and non-prosecution of crime discussed above. As long as offenders are honest about the crime which they have committed, these studies are capable of providing an objective, accurate picture of who commits crime, directly from offenders, and regardless of whether those offenders have ever been arrested, charged or convicted of their offence.

Self-report studies were first carried out in the 1940s and became increasingly popular among criminologists in the 1950s and 1960s, especially in the USA. However, such studies have also been carried out more recently in the UK. For example, Graham and Bowling's Home Office study from 1995 undertook a self-report study (the Youth Lifestyles Survey) with a sample of young people aged between 14 and 25, finding that:

- offending generally was common, with around a third of 22- to 25-year-olds admitting to having committed a criminal offence in the previous year;

- men were far more likely to admit to offending than women;

- frequent offending was fairly rare, with 25 percent of admitted offences being admitted to by only 3 percent of offenders; and

- serious offending was also rare, with only 7 percent admitting to the most serious offences asked about.

A more wide-ranging self-report study was the Offending, Crime and Justice Survey (Budd et al., 2005), again organised by the Home Office, and conducted every year in England and Wales between 2003 and 2006. The OCJS included a sample of 12,000 people between the ages of 10 and 65, and attempted to reveal the extent of low-level antisocial behaviour as well as more serious offences such as theft, burglary and violence. As with Graham and Bowling's earlier study, the OCJS found that the peak age of offending was between 14 and 16, that a significant number of young people aged between 10 and 25 (22 percent) admitted to committing at least one criminal offence in the previous year, and that a small minority of 10- to 25-year-olds (4 percent) committed a disproportionately large number of offences (32 percent of the total).

✎ EXAM TIP

When discussing key self-report studies, make sure that you include details about the study's methodology (e.g. who was included in the study in terms of age, gender, race and so on), and make sure that you approach methodological issues critically rather than offering a straightforward narrative description of how the study was carried out.

Be critical

You need to assess the validity of a range of criticisms which have been directed at self-report studies in the past, in order to analyse their ability to explain who commits crime in depth. For example, you could note that self-report studies have been criticised not only for asking about too many crimes generally and too many insignificant, low-level crimes in particular (as the OCJS arguably did by focusing on 'antisocial behaviour' as well as crime, despite there being no clear definition of what antisocial behaviour actually is), but also for not asking about crime which is more serious but less likely to be the focus of public concern – the 'hidden' crime which tends to be committed by the powerful in society, such as domestic violence, organised crime and large-scale fraud.

Other problems frequently faced by self-report studies, as noted by Box (1981), are:

■ Representativeness – does the sample of people involved in the self-report study, and the offending which they admit to, match offending rates in the wider population? For example, many self-report studies (such as the Youth Lifestyles Survey discussed above) focus on a particular social group, such as young people, and therefore inevitably conclude that this particular group is responsible for a disproportionately high amount of crime, while overlooking the activities of other, less-accessible groups.

■ Confusion – some self-report studies have encountered problematic overlaps between categories of offence, which in turn can lead to confused or inaccurate reports from offenders. Alternatively, categories of offending can be vague – asking about offending 'in the previous six months' will not allow differentiation between people who offend only once every six months and people who offend daily.

■ Comparability – different studies have different questions and different approaches to measuring offending, making them very difficult to compare with each other and generalise from to build up a more complete picture of offenders.

 Make your answer stand out

Read Steven Box (1981) for an extended critique of the methodology of self-report studies, which includes more detailed arguments based around each of the points identified above – but don't forget to question whether this source assumes too much bias in the construction and measurement methods within self-report studies on the part of the powerful people in society who organise them.

The criticisms above are focused on methodological problems in self-report studies, but even a study which succeeded in overcoming these obstacles would not be guaranteed to portray an accurate picture of who commits crime. It is possible that respondents might not be truthful about the nature or extent of the crime which they have committed. In other words, they might underestimate their offending so as to avoid blame or censure, or even overestimate their offending in order to make themselves appear 'tough' or powerful. Alternatively, respondents might not be able to remember their offending accurately, especially if the study asks them to think back over an extended period of time such as several years. If this occurs, the picture of offenders will again be inaccurate.

KEY THEORIST

David Farrington and the Cambridge Study in Delinquency

David Farrington and his colleagues at Cambridge University have provided the most detailed and comprehensive attempt to overcome the criticisms of both official statistics on offenders and smaller-scale self-report studies in the form of the Cambridge Study in Delinquency. The Study began in 1961 by contacting around 400 males from South London when they were aged 8 or 9 years old. Since then, the Study has traced this group of people throughout their lives, noting not only how often they offended (using self-report techniques) but also how often they were arrested, charge and convicted for their criminal behaviour, as well as recording other key life events such as unemployment, the extent and quality of education, and starting a family. The Study has also included measurement of internal factors, such as levels of intelligence, empathy and impulsivity.

A series of key patterns and trends have emerged from the Cambridge Study in terms of who commits crime (Piquero et al., 2007):

- Offending is most likely to take place in the mid-teenage years of a person's life.

- People who start offending at an early age (under the age of 10 for example) tend to continue offending for longer than people who start offending later in life.

- A small sub-group of the sample have been responsible for a disproportionately large amount of the total amount of crime caused by the group.

EXAM TIP

You need to emphasise the multifaceted and innovative approach of the Cambridge Study when explaining what makes it stand out in an exam answer – not just in terms of its longitudinal nature and extended research duration, but also in terms of its attempts to balance internal/psychological and external/environmental factors in explaining why offending occurs and who is responsible for it.

Although the Cambridge Study has produced similar findings to other self-report studies on criminal behaviour (see above), it has emphasised the importance of early intervention in a person's life to prevent crime more than other self-report studies on a smaller scale. This has led writers such as David Farrington to advocate a risk assessment-based approach to identifying who commits crime, prioritising such measures as parent education and training as well as pre-school programmes to ensure that children who are identified as being at risk of becoming offenders are targeted with extra support in the first few years of their lives. The Cambridge Study has claimed that its methods are able to identify the majority of offenders before they reach school age.

Be critical

Give your critical analysis of the Cambridge Study's methodology added depth by citing criminologists such as Jock Young. Young has criticised the Study for overemphasising individual and psychological factors, which could be apparent at a very young age, over societal causes of offending such as unemployment and poverty, which would emerge later in a young person's life, in mid-adolescence and young adulthood.

REVISION NOTE

Read the discussion of the Cambridge Study together with the discussion of biological and psychological positivism as an explanation for crime in Chapters 6 and 7, and with the discussion of the implications of risk assessment for criminal punishment in Chapter 10.

Make your answer stand out

Critically discuss Piquero et al. (2007) as a summary and analysis of the large amount of offender data produced by the Cambridge Study, in terms of its psychological, risk-based approach to explaining crime – you should also contrast this approach with the more radical explanations for crime discussed in Chapter 1 above and in Chapter 9 below.

The Cambridge Study's approach to investigating who offends, and who is likely to offend in the future, has been criticised for taking an approach to the causation of crime and the identification of offenders which is too 'black and white'. In other words, this approach uses characteristics associated with previous offenders to label people (especially very young children) as future offenders, identifying people as 'offenders' without giving enough consideration to their individual circumstances – failing to acknowledge that people's future (offending) behaviour can be very difficult to predict accurately. Finally, Haines and Drakeford have argued that as the study was begun in the early 1960s, it answers more questions about who committed crime then (and why) than it does about who commits crime now.

 Make your answer stand out

McAra and McVie (2010) is a report from another longitudinal self-report study carried out in Scotland, which appears to show that children can move into, and away from, offending behaviour far later in their lives than the Cambridge Study claims, and places more emphasis on social influences on criminal behaviour than the Cambridge Study does.

■ The influence of knowledge about who commits crime on criminal justice policy

In England and Wales successive governments have been heavily influenced by the different methods of offender profiling discussed in this chapter. The Home Office White Paper *Criminal Justice: The way ahead* (2001) published by the New Labour government based large parts of its policy initiatives on the following assertions, all of which were derived from the results of the Offender Index, the Cambridge Study, other self-report studies and prison surveys:

■ There were about a million active offenders in the population at any one time.

■ There was a sub-group of 100,000 offenders who were responsible for a disproportionately large amount of the crime committed.

■ These persistent offenders shared various characteristics in common, such as starting to offend at an early age, using drugs, spending time in care as children, having a poor education, and being unemployed.

The policy results of these assertions were a range of initiatives designed to tackle the link between social exclusion and criminal behaviour, often aimed at intervening in the lives of very young children by offering help to parents (Sure Start) or attempting to improve poor communities by investing money in them (Neighbourhood Renewal), in the belief that, as most crime appears to be committed by the poor and disadvantaged, such policies would reduce crime as well as reducing social exclusion itself. Similar assumptions can be found in the criminal justice policies developed by the Coalition government that took power following the 2010 general election; they revolved around the idea of crime being caused primarily by a 'broken' part of society characterised by single-parent families and those so dependent on welfare that they falsely claim benefits. Again, this approach links crime with poverty, although it places more emphasis on 'problem populations' making the voluntary choice to be poor and to be offenders than New Labour policies did. It is therefore clear that the limited picture of who commits crime portrayed by the sources in this chapter continues to have a disproportionately large influence on criminal justice policy in England and Wales.

✎ EXAM TIP

Critique the relationship between offender profiling and criminal justice policy by arguing that self-report studies have generally tended to focus upon the types of crime which lower-class people tend to commit (such as theft and burglary) when trying to explain who commits crime generally, but have ignored other harmful types of behaviour which are officially defined as criminal, but often not considered to be criminal by the public (such as the fraudulent practices of deliberately misselling mortgages or falsely claiming work-related expenses) – crimes which tend to be committed by middle-class and upper-class people, not the socially excluded. This approach then justifies an argument that much of what we think we know about who commits crime is based around a falsely overstated link between poverty and crime.

■ Putting it all together

Answer guidelines

See the essay question at the start of the chapter.

Approaching the question

This question is asking you to examine the strength of the evidence indicating a link between being young and committing crime. The question would require you to go beyond considering the influence of age on the commission of crime, in order to look at other individual and social factors which might be more influential on the commission of crime than age is.

Important points to include

- Introduction mapping out the overall structure of the essay in brief.
- Identification of evidence indicating the importance of the link between age and who is most likely to commit crime – for example, the OCJS statement that the peak age of offending is between 14 and 16 years old, government policies which have supported this assertion under New Labour and Coalition governments.

▶

- Identification of evidence which contradicts this view – for example, the Offender Index shows that only 5 percent of those convicted in court are children.
- Identification of other factors which might have a greater influence of who commits crime than age in terms of individual factors – for example, the Cambridge Study's focus on personality type and low IQ.
- Identification of other factors which might have a greater influence of who commits crime than age in terms of social factors – for example critical criminology's focus on the hidden relationship between wealth and crime
- Conclusions summarising the essay's arguments and explaining the essay's position on the claim in the question.

 Make your answer stand out

- Be critical of the assertion that official statistics and research can tell us everything there is to know about who commits crime, in terms of knowledge about crime which is not committed because of poverty.
- When discussing particular self-report studies, show knowledge of how these studies were constructed, and don't be afraid to critique their methodological weaknesses.
- Pay particular attention to the strengths and weaknesses of the longitudinal Cambridge Study in terms of what it tells us about who commits crime and how much influence its risk-based and positivist assumptions have had (and should have had) on criminal justice policy in England and Wales.

READ TO IMPRESS

Box, S. (1981) *Deviance, Reality and Society* (2nd edn) London: Holt, Rinehart and Wilson.

Budd, T., Sharp, C. and Mayhew, P. (2005) *Offending in England and Wales: First results from the Crime and justice survey,* Home Office Research Study no. 275, London: Home Office.

Flood-Page, C., Campbell, S., Harrington, V. and Miller, J. (2000) *Youth Crime: Findings from the 1998/99 youth lifestyles survey,* Home Office Research Study no. 209, London: Home Office.

McAra, L. and McVie, S. (2010) 'Youth Crime and Justice: Key messages from the Edinburgh study of youth transitions and crime', *Criminal Justice and Criminology,* **10**(2): 179–209.

Piquero, A.R, Farrington, D.P. and Blumstein, A. (2007), *Key Issues in Criminal Career Research: New analyses of the Cambridge study in delinquent development,* Cambridge: Cambridge University Press.

www.pearsoned.co.uk/lawexpress

Go online to access more revision support, including quizzes to test your knowledge, sample questions with answer guidelines, podcasts you can download and more!

Crime and the media

4

Revision checklist

Essential points you should know:

- [ ] How (and how accurately) the different forms of media portray crime and offenders
- [ ] What is known about the effects of media images of crime and offenders as a cause of crime
- [ ] What is known about the effect of media images of crime and offenders as a cause of public fear of crime
- [ ] The idea of 'moral panics' and the evidence for their existence
- [ ] Differences in media coverage of different types of crime

■ Topic map

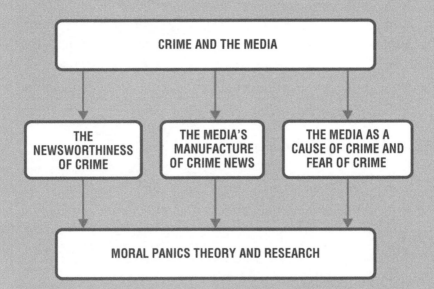

■ Introduction

The extent, and accuracy, of the information which the media produce about crime is a vital area of criminological study.

The nature of media in today's society is more complex and diverse than ever before. Media information can now be sent around the world almost instantaneously and, as a result, is a constant presence in everyday life. More importantly for criminologists, the media are where many people derive what they know (or think they know) about the nature and extent of crime, and crime is an essential element of both factual and fictional media coverage.

ASSESSMENT ADVICE

Essay and exam questions on the media and crime can take a variety of forms, but several key themes can be identified. Firstly, there is the issue of how, and how accurately, the media represents the nature and extent of crime and whether the media's manufacturing of crime-related information represents particular social interests and/or marginalises certain social groups. Secondly, there is the question of whether the media is capable of actually causing crime (and fear of crime) through the ways in which it portrays different crime types, especially violence. The question of whether the media is capable of generating 'moral panics' about a particular crime-related topic is a variant of this topic. Thirdly, there is the issue of whether factual and fictional portrayals of crime in the media have the same impact on those who experience them.

■ Sample question

Could you answer this question? Below is a typical essay question that could arise on this topic. Guidelines on answering the question are included at the end of this chapter. Another sample question and guidance on tackling it can be found on the companion website.

ESSAY QUESTION

Critically discuss the view that criminology has proved that the media not only distorts the reality of crime, but is also capable of causing crime directly.

■ Key sources, theorists and theories in crime and media studies

---

KEY THEORY

The 'newsworthiness' of crime

Just as crime does not become crime until it is labelled as such by someone with the power to do so, so social events do not become news until the media selects it as news. Writers such as Steve Chibnall have tried to identify the characteristics which the media look for when selecting events as 'news'.

- Chibnall identified a range of different characteristics which made events newsworthy, such as immediacy (fast-moving or topical stories), novelty (a new angle on a particular crime-related issue), titillation (scandalous or taboo stories) and personalisation (stories about celebrities), individual causes of crime rather than wider social problems, and proximity between an event and its audience.

- Later writers have built on Chibnall's framework – Yvonne Jewkes, for example, emphasises the **newsworthiness** of stories relating to risk, vulnerability and victimisation, and Chris Greer argues that stories which can be portrayed visually, through images, are more likely to be selected as news.

✎ EXAM TIP

Try to relate the different academic perspectives on newsworthiness back to theoretical ideas on how and why news is produced. There are three key approaches which you could use in this context:

- radical approaches which focus on the state's ability to control the public's ideas about crime through the media (either through monolithic control or through hegemony given the advantageous position of state-run criminal justice agencies in defining crime and crime news);
- liberal pluralist approaches which emphasise the ability and autonomy of journalists to resist the news-making pressures of the powerful and report news objectively; and
- postmodern approaches which reject both of the previous theories in favour of emphasising the fragmented, diversified nature of the modern mass media, in which crime news objectivity is impossible and the public play a key part in shaping news through their participation in Internet sites such as Twitter and Facebook.

Make your answer stand out

Read and cite Hall et al. (1978) for an example of the radical perspective on news construction which argues that the state has a great deal of influence over the manufacture of crime-related news, in terms of the media's reproduction of the values belonging to those with enough power to use the media in this way. This study also claims that crime stories involving violence take priority over other types of crime in the media. Hall et al.'s study is also a classic example of the literature on the creation and maintenance of moral panics, a topic which is discussed in more detail later in this chapter. To add further analytical depth, you could compare and contrast Hall et al.'s study with the work of Ericson (1991) or Schlesinger and Tumber (1994), both of which argue that the production of crime news involves more negotiation, conflict and diversity among a range of individuals and agencies than the work of Hall et al. suggests, while acknowledging the power of the state to manipulate the media for its own ends and interests.

! Don't be tempted to . . .

A basic error in student exam answers on media-related topics is to treat the media as being one homogenous source of information on crime, with shared values and interests. In fact, the media is more diverse and complex than ever before, including such social institutions as television, radio, newspapers and the Internet, and mobile phone technology in the forms of apps, and you should always take care to reflect this when discussing how the media can report, distort and cause criminality.

KEY SOURCE

Content analysis research on how the media portray crime

A wide range of research has been carried out into how the media represent the nature and extent of crime, and how these accounts differ from other sources of knowledge on crime, such as police and British Crime Survey statistics. A common way of doing this type of research is **content analysis** – counting how many stories involving crime generally (or a specific type of crime) appear in an element of the media over a given period of time, or counting how many times a particular word, phrase or image appears. This can be done quantitatively (counting up frequencies), qualitatively (looking at the context of reporting and the meanings behind it) or both.

Although there is a large quantity of this type of research, Sparks (1992) shows that some general patterns can be identified, bearing in mind that research has found variations according to place and media type:

- Crime and criminal justice are regular, constant features of both factual and fictional mass media portrayals, in the UK and elsewhere.

- Crime-related stories have become more and more frequent in the factual and fictional mass media since the mid-twentieth century (particularly in newspapers), with tabloids reporting more often on specific criminal offences than broadsheets.

- Violence (particularly homicide and rape) is over-represented in newspapers and television news, as well as fictional sources such as books and films, compared with what is known about its incidence in official crime statistics; property offences are correspondingly under-represented.

- Offenders reported on in the media tend to be considerably older and of higher social status than the average offender in crime statistics.

- The mass media have increasingly focused upon victims of crime in their crime-related output over the past 30 years or so, with women tending to be over-represented as victims in both factual and fictional sources.

- Factual and fictional reports tend to use individual explanations rather than social explanations for crime, and tend to focus on specific, discrete incidents rather than general crime trends.

- Although criminal justice agencies such as the police are generally portrayed positively in factual and fictional media, they are portrayed more critically than they were in the mid-twentieth century, and the reported clear-up rate for crime is therefore declining in both factual and fictional media portrayals of crime.

Be critical

You need to challenge the claims to reliability and objectivity made by quantitative content analysis in essay and exam answers. These criticisms need to be included not only when critically analysing content analysis generally, but also when evaluating the results of specific content analysis studies in your answer. You could criticise this type of study, for example, for giving the appearance of objectivity in analysing the media when in fact the categories which form the framework for the counting process are subjective, carry hidden meaning in themselves and can therefore distort the results of analysis.

Content analysis can also overlook differences between different types (e.g. television news) and sub-types (e.g. local and national television news) of media, and between different geographical locations. Finally, the same word or image as represented in the media can mean a range of different things to different people, depending on the media type and how the 'receiver' sees themselves in relation to those in the factual or fictional story.

These criticisms reveal the fallacy of claiming that media content analysis can be purely objective.

 Make your answer stand out

Refer to Sparks (1992) for a detailed critical analysis of quantitative content analysis-based research into crime fiction, and a discussion of how this type of analysis can increase the public's fear of crime.

KEY THEORY

The criminogenic media

Criminologists the media have argued that causes crime in a number of ways, which include:

- labelling, where the media label a particular type of activity as criminal – media reports on drug-taking, for example, led Jock Young to conclude that the media had played a key part in the increased criminal justice repression of drug use in the UK in the early 1970s;

- providing the means for crime, through transmitting knowledge or techniques relating to the commission of crime which offenders can then use, or through arousing, desensitising or glamorising crime in a way which affects people's behaviour – Bandura's research which linked the viewing of a violent film on television with increased violence and aggression in real life is an example of behavioural research in this field; or

- providing physical opportunities for crime, through opportunities to commit various offences via access to the Internet, or through encouraging a consumerist ethos via the advertising of desirable goods such as iPads and games consoles, which in turn encourages theft to acquire these goods.

Other writers have argued that the media also increases the public's fear of crime:

- Gerbner's 'cultivation analysis' has claimed that there is a link between heavy television watching and increased fear of crime in the USA, due to increased association of the over-emphasis of violence on television with reality.

- In the UK, Schlesinger's research found that women in the UK were more sensitive to images of violent crime on television programmes which heavily over-represented violence, such as *Crimewatch*, and Williams and Dickenson found a significant relationship between disproportionate fear of crime and reading newspapers which emphasised violent crime, even when social status, gender and age were controlled for.

Be critical

In essay and exam answers, you need to focus your analysis on critically discussing the extent to which this type of study is capable of proving that the crime or the fear really are caused by the media, as opposed to another social factor.

Bandura's research, for example, which was discussed above, could not conclusively prove that it was watching the violent film which caused the violent behaviour later, as opposed to other social, environmental or psychological factors affecting the viewers. In other, similar studies, it is difficult to prove the direction of the relationship between watching violence and violent behaviour – in other words, the relationship could be explained by people who are already violent choosing to watch violent programmes, rather than being made violent by those programmes. Other criticisms of this 'effects research' on crime and the fear of crime are that:

- it tends to do research in artificial situations, rather than natural, realistic scenarios;

- it tends to research short-term effects rather than long-term ones;

- it does not define 'violence' in enough detail, or do enough to distinguish between different types of violence in the media (Sparks, 1992).

✎ EXAM TIP

Although it is generally accepted that the media has some effect on crime and the fear of crime, you should still be selective in the 'effects research' which you cite in an exam answer. Rather than limiting your discussion to quantitative research which claims to prove a direct link between media consumption and violence, choose research which has a partly qualitative approach and which acknowledges that people interpret the media subjectively, and in a way which reflects their own experiences of crime and other social structures.

Make your answer stand out

Ditton et al.'s (2004) study into the effects of the media on crime and the fear of crime is one which blends quantitative and qualitative research, and emphasises that different people interpret different aspects of the media in different ways, concluding that the relationship between crime, fear of crime and media experience is present, but far from direct.

KEY THEORY

Moral panics

The concept of **moral panic** is most closely associated with the work of Stan Cohen. In his study of the clashes between Mods and Rockers in the UK in the mid-1960s, Cohen argued that powerful societal groups defined these groups of young people, and their behaviour, as a threat to society, or 'folk devil' in the public's imagination. The media then simplified the threat for public consumption, triggering off a disproportionate, irrational and rapid increase in levels of public concern – a 'moral panic' – about the groups and what they were doing.

Criminal justice authorities then responded to the public panic with repressive measures, such as more intensive policing and harsher court sentencing. In this way, the cycle of 'deviancy amplification' by the media, containing processes of exaggeration and distortion of events, prediction of worse problems to come, and symbolisation of the characteristics of those labelled as criminogenic (e.g. hairstyles or clothes) continued until the panic subsided, or social changes relating to the targeted behaviour occurred. Cohen argued that moral panics were inherently volatile, and could disappear as suddenly as they appeared.

The works discussed above by Hall et al. and Young are other examples of criminological research into the existence and effects of media-driven moral panics.

Be critical

Show the flaws in the moral panic approach by arguing that it is difficult to prove that a media and public reaction to a social issue is disproportionate, because it is almost impossible to know what a rational, proportionate response would be at any given time. Do not be afraid to argue, in essays and exams, that the moral element in moral panics has not been fully explained or defined by those researching them.

Moral panic theorists have been criticised, especially by left realist criminologists, for:

- assuming that fear of crime generated by moral panic is groundless and not to be taken seriously;
- overstating the panic in the response of the media; and
- oversimplifying both the nature of deviance targeted by moral panics, and the readiness of the public to respond to moral panics generated by the media.

A more recent area of criticism has been Cohen's assertion that moral panics are uncommon in society. In the current media climate, moral panics seem to be a regular occurrence, and are manipulated by the media and business to generate sales and profit for themselves. Those who have been labelled as 'folk devils' now also have the ability to respond actively to their labelling with their own views and arguments, through social networking websites for example.

 Make your answer stand out

Make sure that you read and cite the most recent version of Cohen's work on moral panics (Cohen, 2002), so that you can include his responses to the criticisms of moral panic theory which are outlined in the 'Be critical' box above.

! Don't be tempted to . . .

The moral panic concept is an easy one to use inaccurately in an exam answer due to its great influence on criminology, so make sure that you apply the concepts developed by Cohen and other key writers clearly and precisely to show your deep understanding of this issue, rather than dropping the phrase 'moral panic' into an answer without explanation or context.

■ The crime – media relationship's influence on criminal justice policy

Crime and criminal justice have been, and continue to be, crucial issues for media coverage, and so a wide range of related topics selected and amplified by media coverage have influenced criminal justice policy. However, to allow you to make your essay and exam answers as topical as possible, this part of the chapter deals with two twenty-first-century crime-media issues in policy terms: the Internet and cybercrime, and the response to terrorism.

■ Focusing on cybercrime first, the Internet is now a hugely popular element of the mass media in its own right, but the cybercrime which it has provided opportunities for committing has greatly influenced criminal justice policy in the UK.

■ The problem of cyber-pornography, for example influenced the expansion of the range of sexual offences in the Sexual Offences Act 2003, to include offences relating to the grooming of children for the purpose of committing sexual offences later, and also triggered the high-profile police operation 'Operation Ore' in 2002, while the criminal activity of paedophiles more generally has triggered off waves of media campaigns to allow communities to find out the whereabouts of offenders in their area, and the introduction of policy partially allowing the release of this information in 2009; while the apparently significant increase in Internet-based credit card fraud was a key influence on the simplification and expansion of fraud law (to include e.g. defrauding a cash machine with fraudulently obtained credit card details) in the Fraud Act 2006.

■ In the response to terrorism, the worldwide media broadcasting of the images of the destruction of the World Trade Centre twin towers in New York on 11 September 2001 were used both as encouragement for further fundamentalist attacks (various insurgent groups have regularly transmitted broadcasts, and even live executions, via the Internet since then) and as a way of stirring up public revulsion and support for military responses in Iraq and Afghanistan.

■ The terrorist attacks of 11 September and 7 July 2005 in London generated a wide range of anti-terrorist legislation in the UK, such as the Prevention of Terrorism Act 2005 and the Counter-Terrorism Act 2008, which have increased police powers to stop, search and interrogate those suspected of terrorism, and have also played a part in the great expansion of CCTV use in the UK, now alleged to have the most CCTV cameras anywhere in the world.

✎ EXAM TIP

Try to link discussion of the media's links to cybercrime and terrorism to wider academic criminology 'risk management' debates on whether recent criminal justice policy developments in these areas have led to an increased fear of crime and of those considered as 'outsiders' in contemporary society.

■ Putting it all together

Answer guidelines

See the essay question at the start of the chapter.

Approaching the question

This question is asking you to do two things – firstly, to assess the extent to which the media misrepresents the nature and extent of crime, and, secondly, to assess the extent to which the media can be said to cause crime in its own right. The question needs reference to the key academic writers and debates, but also provides you with the scope to relate current crime-related issues featuring in the media to established academic theories and concepts.

Important points to include

■ Introduction briefly showing awareness of the complex nature of media in today's society and mapping out the rest of the essay.

■ Theories and research critically analysing the media's potential misreporting of crime – 'the newsworthiness' of crime and criminal justice, different perspectives on the ways in which the media manufacture crime-based news, the strengths and weaknesses of content analysis on media reporting of crime.

■ Theories and research critically analysing the media's potential causation of crime and fear of crime – the moral panic concept and its application in today's society, the reliability of 'media effects' research on crime and fear of crime, perspectives on how the media might provide means and opportunities for different types of crime.

■ Conclusion drawing together arguments on whether both parts of the statement in the question can be proved true.

 Make your answer stand out

■ Critically analyse older crime-media research (such as Cohen's moral panic theory) by applying it to contemporary research evidence on how the media report crime and criminal justice issues.

- Show awareness of a range of perspectives on the media's reporting of crime, including the hegemonic, pluralist and postmodern theories, rather than restricting discussion to one particular approach.
- Choose the most reliable, balanced research on media effects – research that combines quantitative and qualitative approaches – rather than dismissing the effects on the media on crime on the basis of less reliable research.

READ TO IMPRESS

Cohen, S. (2002) *Folk Devils and Moral Panics* (3rd edn), London: Routledge.

Ditton, J., Chadee, D., Farrall, S., Gilchrist, E. and Bannister, J. (2004) 'From Imitation to Intimidation: A note on the curious and changing relationship between the media, crime and fear of crime', *British Journal of Criminology,* **44**(4): 595–610.

Ericson, R. (1991) 'Mass Media, Crime, Law and Justice', *British Journal of Criminology,* **31**(3): 219–49.

Hall, S., Critchley, C., Jefferson, T., Clarke, J. and Roberts, B. (1978) *Policing the Crisis,* London: Macmillan.

Schlesinger, P. and Tumber, H. (1994) *Reporting Crime,* Oxford: Oxford University Press.

Sparks, R. (1992) *Television and the Drama of Crime,* Buckingham: Open University Press.

Thompson, K. (1998) *Moral Panics,* London: Routledge.

www.pearsoned.co.uk/lawexpress

 Go online to access more revision support, including quizzes to test your knowledge, sample questions with answer guidelines, podcasts you can download, and more!

Classicist criminology

5

Revision checklist

Essential points you should know:

☐ The key principles of classicism in relation to explaining why crime occurs and the strengths and weaknesses of these ideas

☐ The arguments of the main classicist criminological writers, such as Cesare Beccaria, Travis Hirschi and the situational crime prevention theorists

☐ The strengths and weaknesses of classicist criminology in terms of how well it explains crime

☐ The extent to which classicism still influences modern-day explanations for crime and criminal justice policy

■Topic map

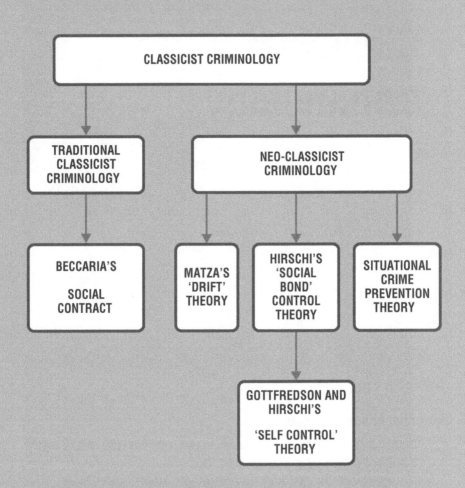

■ Introduction

Classicism was the earliest systematic, rational approach to explaining crime and punishment.

Before classicism emerged in the mid-eighteenth century, crime was seen in many societies as the result of sin, and therefore as the work of the devil. As a result, the state claimed the right to inflict a wide range of often cruel and violent physical punishments on criminals, in the name of punishing sins against God. Criminal justice was frequently biased, inconsistent and vulnerable to rulers' changes of mind. Thinking on crime and punishment began to change during the eighteenth century, as part of the philosophical movement known as the Enlightenment, which believed in the power of human beings to decide on how they behaved for themselves. Although the first classicist writers, such as Cesare Beccaria, were more concerned with methods of punishment than with why people committed crime in itself, their ideas became influential in terms of explaining crime as well, and continue to be important in this context today.

ASSESSMENT ADVICE

Remember that classicism was originally more about fair methods of punishment than explaining why crime occurred. So, for essay and exam questions, be prepared to discuss not only the original ideas of writers such as Beccaria, but also the ways in which classicist thought has influenced more modern-day criminological theories.

■ Sample question

Could you answer this question? Below is a typical essay question that could arise on this topic. Guidelines on answering the question are included at the end of this chapter. Another sample question and guidance on tackling it can be found on the companion website.

ESSAY QUESTION

Critically discuss the idea that classicist theories have been the most effective theory in terms of explaining crime.

■ Key theorists and theories in classicist criminology

KEY DEFINITION: Classicist criminology

A set of ideas which argues that crime is the result of individuals' voluntary decisions to offend, having weighed up the advantages and disadvantages of committing crime rationally.

🕮 REVISION NOTE

Positivism and classicism can appear together as part of a 'compare and contrast' exam question, because they are often thought of as being completely opposite to each other in terms of explaining why people commit crime. Therefore, make sure that you revise the material on positivism in Chapters 6 and 7 alongside the material in this chapter. In particular, pay close attention to the discussion of the similarities and differences between positivism and classicism in Chapter 6, to test your understanding of how well classicism explains crime.

KEY THEORIST

Cesare Beccaria

Beccaria was an Enlightenment philosopher who believed that people were fully responsible for their own actions. Beccaria argued that a 'social contract' existed, of which all members of society formed a part. Under this social contract, each person had to give up a part of his or her freedom to do as they liked, so that a universal 'lesser freedom' could be achieved for everyone. The criminal law's job was then to punish those who broke the terms of this social contract by committing crime, which gave them an unfair advantage over the rest of society. It was these beliefs on how punishment for crime should work which led to Beccaria's arguments about why crime itself occurred. Beccaria believed that individuals were free-willed, capable of rational thought and therefore responsible for their own actions, including crime. Criminals, therefore, made the voluntary and free-willed choice to commit crime, having weighed up the potential advantages and disadvantages of doing so, and decided that the pros outweighed the cons. Beccaria therefore saw criminals as 'moral calculators' who could be prevented from committing further criminal behaviour by punishment which acted as a deterrent, and made the disadvantages of committing crime outweigh the advantages and pleasure associated with breaking the law.

KEY THEORIST

Jeremy Bentham

Bentham built on Beccaria's ideas by arguing that punishment should aim to achieve the greatest amount of happiness for the greatest number of people in society, and should be measured so as to ensure that the pain of the punishment outweighed the pleasure gained by committing crime. This approach is known as utilitarianism. It depends on the principle that each person is responsible for the crimes which they commit, and therefore is capable of being deterred by punishment, so that they will not reoffend.

Be critical

You should think about how classicism ignored the fact that offenders could be very different from one another, and therefore ignored the fact that it could be these differences between offenders which might explain crime rather than rational choice – in your view, to what extent can individual (physical, biological or psychological) differences explain criminal behaviour? Beccaria's approach treated everyone as being equally responsible for their crimes, regardless of whether they were children or adults, sane or insane, and so on – you could argue that this is too harsh on those who we would normally say were not fully responsible for their criminal actions, such as those with serious mental illness.

Beccaria also overlooked the fact that not all crime is the subject of 'moral calculation' of its advantages and disadvantages. Some crimes are committed accidentally, or on the spur of the moment, rather than being planned (e.g. because the offender is drunk, or mentally ill), so it could be argued that the classicist approach does not fully explain why people commit crime.

KEY THEORY

David Matza, Travis Hirschi and control theory

The criminological theory known as control theory was primarily driven by classicist beliefs in freedom of choice and the ability of each individual to prevent themselves from committing crime. David Matza pointed out that many people stop committing crime in their late teens or early twenties, even though their social circumstances remain the same. Matza therefore argued that offenders drift in and out of criminal behaviour,

▶

justifying their offending by making the decision to rationalise their behaviour in their own minds, and to neutralise law-abiding societal values temporarily. Matza identified a series of '**techniques of neutralisation**' used by offenders to justify their behaviour to themselves and others, such as denying responsibility for their actions. Matza's approach is clearly linked to the idea of classicism, because it relies on the view that offenders make the voluntary decision to 'switch off' conventional values in order to make committing crime easier, and so make the decision to start – and to stop ∟ committing crime.

Travis Hirschi's work was focused on the reasons why people do *not* commit crime. Hirschi concluded that crime was normal behaviour, and that everyone would commit crime if there was nothing to stop them doing so – a belief in voluntary freedom of choice to commit crime which was clearly influenced by classicist criminology. Hirschi further claimed that four factors were influential in people's decisions not to commit crime. These were attachment (caring about what others thought, such as parents), commitment (commitment to achieving conventional success, such as a good education), involvement (involvement with behaving conventionally) and belief (belief that society's rules, including the law, should be obeyed). Hirschi's **control theory** therefore related to social bonds – the stronger a person's links were to the conventional social order, the less likely that person would be to commit crime.

! Don't be tempted to . . .

Although Hirschi's theory is clearly influenced by classicism, do not argue that it is purely classicist in nature. There is a sociological influence on Hirschi's ideas too. This influence is clearly visible in his emphasis on features of conventional societal behaviour (such as attachment to family). Note also that Hirschi does not use terms such as 'attachment' and 'belief' in the same way as a psychologist would; again, his approach is more sociological than individualist or classicist in this sense.

EXAM TIP

If you are asked to discuss Hirschi's control theory critically, in terms of explaining its strengths and weaknesses, you could point out that one of the theory's weaknesses is that Hirschi's research findings only covered young males. It could be argued that this issue weakens the reliability of Hirschi's theory.

Be critical

Criticism of Matza's work can be related to the importance of basing theories on hard empirical evidence – you should question whether he defined 'drift' clearly enough, and also question how this concept can be accurately measured, if at all. In relation to Hirschi's control theory, you should think about how important its ignorance of types of crime which are committed by the powerful in society (such as corporate and white-collar crime) is for its ability to explain crime generally – how important and frequent are these types of crime, according to available evidence?

Hirschi's theory can also be challenged on other grounds such as:

■ not explaining what sort of crime, or how much crime, people will commit if they were not controlled by social bonds;

■ assuming that everyone would automatically commit crime if they were not restrained from doing so by social bonds.

KEY THEORY

Gottfredson and Hirschi's 'self-control' control theory

Gottfredson and Hirschi's theory attempted to explain all types of crime, including corporate and white-collar crime. This theory was significantly different from Hirschi's earlier work. For Gottfredson and Hirschi, most crime was trivial, unplanned and aimed at obtaining short-term excitement. Criminal behaviour was therefore due to a high level of personal irresponsibility, and an inability to plan ahead in life or delay gratification.

As a result, Gottfredson and Hirschi argued that there were two key factors in understanding why crime was committed – a person's level of internal self-control, and the presence of opportunities to commit crime. In this theory, bonds with society did not explain why crime occurred. Once socialisation had occurred within a person's family, it was the internal ability to resist the temptation to commit crime which was important.

Be critical

Use writers who are critical of Gottfredson and Hirschi's classicist approach to add depth to your criticism of this theory. Consider and critically analyse the arguments of writers such as Jock Young, who:

■ criticises self-control theory for oversimplifying the reasons why crime is committed (because they claimed that their theory explained every type of crime);

►

- overemphasises the importance of poor parenting in terms of why people have low self-control, at the expense of other potential reasons for lack of restraint, such as mental illness or alcohol abuse;
- does not fully explain how different types of opportunity can affect the nature and frequency of criminal behaviour.

Gottfredson and Hirschi further argued that a person's ability to show self-control was developed in childhood, that levels of self-control remained stable throughout a person's life, and that the absence of self-control was due to bad or ineffective parenting.

 Make your answer stand out

An important issue relating to control theory is whether Hirschi's first 'social bond' theory and his second 'self-control' theory can really be said to be types of the same theoretical approach. Both approaches are based on the idea that, if there is nothing to stop them, people will naturally commit crime to make things as easy and enjoyable for themselves as possible – a traditional classicist view of crime. As shown above, however, there are significant differences between the two theories. Read the original sources on 'social bond' theory (Hirschi, 1969) and on 'self-control' theory (Gottfredson and Hirschi, 1990) to assess the strengths and weaknesses of both theories, and to achieve a deeper level of critical analysis in relation to the effectiveness and coherence of modern-day classicist theory.

KEY THEORY

Situational crime prevention theory

Situational crime prevention theory focused upon reducing the opportunities for crime in particular practical and geographical situations, on the management and design of the geographical environment where people lived, and upon increasing the risks of offenders being caught. The rationale for this type of approach was that it was easier to make small, practical changes to the environment in order to prevent crime than it was to tackle complex social issues, such as poverty.

The theory, developed by writers such as Ronald Clarke, Derek Cornish and Oscar Newman, was closely linked to research, and its supporters relied on the results of research into particular crime prevention projects as evidence that their theory worked.

- Examples of situational crime prevention in practice have included fitting good quality locks and alarm systems to reduce rates of domestic burglary and the redesigning of tower blocks and housing estates to increase monitoring and prevent offenders from gaining entry.

■ James Wilson and George Kelling argued that in areas where broken windows and graffiti were left unrepaired, public fear of crime increased and offending became more and more common.

■ Another branch of the theory was provided by routine activities theory (developed by Lawrence Cohen, Marcus Felson, and Paul and Patricia Brantingham among others). Routine activities theory argued that crime could be reduced by targeting environmental places where there were likely offenders and suitable targets, but where there was no one capable of guarding against and reporting crime, and making those places safer – in other words, by changing the criminal routines of offenders and discouraging them from committing crime.

Overall, situational crime prevention theorists aimed for a more practical, straightforward approach to explaining crime, but one which also linked back to classicist beliefs about offenders making rational decisions on the basis of weighing up the risks and rewards of committing crime.

✎ **EXAM TIP**

Situational crime prevention has clear links to classicist beliefs about the rationality and free will of offenders, and their calculation of the risks and rewards of crime. But its focus on the environment in which crime is committed also has links back to the Chicago School, which used an environmental and positivistic approach to explaining crime which relied on offenders not having free will to commit crime (see Chapter 8 for more details on the Chicago School). When discussing situational control theory in an essay or exam answer, you could argue that it is theoretically inconsistent, because it mixes together positivist and classicist approaches to criminology which seem to be incompatible with each other.

Be critical

A key criticism of situational theory, reflected in the work of writers such as Sampson and Laub, is that situational control theory does not explain *why* people commit or do not commit crime. In other words, it ignores offenders' motivations for offending, which might be rooted in social causes (such as poverty) rather than the rational calculation of risk. You could question the extent to which this failure to address motive is important in explaining crime – is all crime really rooted in voluntary choice, as situational theorists argue? If it is, the failure to include motivations for offending in situational theory is unimportant. But if you do not believe this is the case, then you can criticise the theory for ignoring individual and social explanations for offending which limit freedom of choice.

Situational control theory has also struggled with the issue of displacement – the process by which offenders, when faced with situational crime prevention measures such as CCTV, will not stop committing crime, but will instead simply move their offending to another place which does not have the same protection.

The theory has also been weakened by its reliance on research which does not always prove that the theory actually works – the ability of CCTV to actually reduce crime has never been conclusively proved, for example. The environmental redesigning which situational control theory recommends can also lead to increased social control and surveillance of public activity (lawful as well as unlawful), the exclusion of certain social groups from formerly public space, as the rich develop their own security defences, and an increase in the public's fear of crime.

Radical writers such as Steve Tombs have even questioned whether situational control theories are a criminological theory at all, or just a state-biased method of managing crime in practice.

■ Classicist criminology's influences on criminal justice policy

Classicist criminology has had a variety of influences on criminal justice policy in practice:

■ Beccaria's emphasis on universal equality, individual responsibility for crime, the effectiveness of deterrence on calculating offenders, and just and proportionate punishment had clear influences on various criminal justice systems in his own time, especially those in the USA and France.

■ The 'self-control' theory developed by Gottfredson and Hirschi focused on the importance of good parenting in preventing crime, and this was one of the inspirations behind the New Labour government's Sure Start and Splash programmes (which targeted parents whose children were seen to be at risk of offending, and offered them help and support) at the start of the twenty-first century.

■ Situational crime prevention theory's 'common sense' approach to explaining why crime occurs, together with its emphasis on research to back the theory up, has proved to be very appealing to politicians who develop criminal justice policy, and has led to its use in a wide variety of practical approaches to preventing crime, both in the UK and in other countries across the world.

■ The rapid growth in the use of CCTV and speed cameras is just one high-profile example of situational control theory at work, and there are many others, such as the encouragement of the public by the government to fit burglar alarms and secure locks in their homes, and the use of steering locks to prevent car theft.

- While these measures have not been conclusively proven to prevent crime every time, they are relatively cheap for governments to implement as part of policy when compared with the costs of tackling social issues like unemployment, easy to understand in terms of their operation and effects, and supported (to some extent) by research.

All of these factors mean that it is highly likely that classicist criminology, particularly in the form of situational crime prevention, will continue to play a key part in criminal justice policy, in the UK and elsewhere.

■ Putting it all together

Answer guidelines

See the essay question at the start of the chapter.

Approaching the question

This question is asking you about how effective classicist criminological theories have been in explaining the motivations for crime. To answer this question fully, you would need to be aware of the evolution of classicist criminology, from Beccaria's original punishment-based theory of crime, through to the modern range of situational crime prevention theories. Through each stage of the theories' development, you would need to keep the focus on effectiveness – in other words, what evidence is there that classicist theories really can explain why crime occurs? Effectiveness can be measured in different ways, so you would need to look at criticisms of the approaches on both the theoretical and the research level.

Important points to include

- Introduction mapping out the overall structure of the essay in brief.
- Statement of the key principles of classicism in general.
- Explanation of Beccaria's ideas, their influence and a critique of their effectiveness.
- Explanation of Hirschi's ideas, their influence and a critique of their effectiveness.
- Explanation of the situational crime prevention theorists' ideas, their influence and a critique of their effectiveness.
- Conclusions summarising the essay's arguments and explaining the essay's position on the effectiveness of classicist criminology in explaining crime.

▶

Make your answer stand out

- Emphasise the inconsistencies within classicist criminology – for example the use of positivist research and theory in the classicist situational control approach, or the differences between Hirschi's earlier and later control theory work.

- Use a range of research which evaluates situational crime prevention strategies in criminal justice practice, and critically analyse the research's methods (i.e. how it was carried out) as well as its results (i.e. to what extent it proves that situational crime prevention really does cut crime).

- Point out links between classicism and other key developments in modern criminology, such as the rise in the 'risk management' of certain problematic individuals and groups in society based on the perceived risk of offending which they pose.

READ TO IMPRESS

Felson, M. and Boba, R. (2010) *Crime and Everyday Life* (4th edn), Thousand Oaks, CA: Sage.

Gottfredson, M. and Hirschi, T. (1990) *A General Theory of Crime,* Stanford, CA: Stanford University Press.

von Hirschi, A., Garland, D. and Wakefield, A. (eds) (2000) *Ethical and Social Perspectives on Situational Crime Prevention,* Oxford: Hart.

Hirschi, T. (1969) *Causes of Delinquency,* Berkeley, CA: University of California Press.

Matza, D. (1964) *Delinquency and Drift,* New York: Wiley.

Roshier, B. (1989) *Controlling Crime: The classical perspective in criminology,* Milton Keynes: Open University Press.

 www.pearsoned.co.uk/lawexpress

Go online to access more revision support, including quizzes to test your knowledge, sample questions with answer guidelines, podcasts you can download, and more!

Biological positivist criminology

6

Revision checklist

Essential points you should know:

☐ The key principles of positivism in relation to explaining why crime occurs

☐ The arguments of the key thinkers in biological positivist criminology, and the strengths and weaknesses of their ideas

☐ The main types of modern-day neo-positivist biological criminological studies, and their respective strengths and weaknesses

☐ The extent to which these biological positivistic explanations for crime still influence modern-day explanations for crime and criminal justice policy

■Topic map

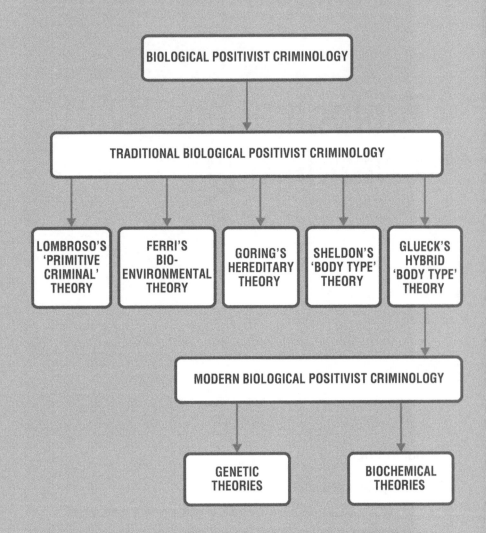

■ Introduction

Biological positivism was the first theory to use the 'appliance of science' to explain the causes of crime. It believed that it could explain why some people commit crime, and therefore how criminals could be reformed or prevented from offending in the first place.

Though many of the original biological approaches to positivist criminology have now been discredited, it has been argued that positivism still influences criminology today – both in the methods it used to research crime and in more modern forms of positivist theory, such as biosocial approaches to explaining crime.

Biological positivist criminology developed as a response to the explanation of crime as a freewill, voluntary decision put forward by classicism (see Chapter 5). More specifically, it emerged as an attempt to explain continued increases in crime rates, despite the introduction of an organised criminal justice response to crime under the influence of classicist beliefs.

There are a number of distinctive features of biological positivist criminology. Firstly, in contrast to classicism, positivist criminology focused on the characteristics of offenders rather than on the offences which offenders had committed. It focused on the idea of offenders as being 'predetermined' to commit crime. In other words, offenders were driven to commit crime by internal factors which were beyond their control. Therefore, positivists believed in treating offenders rather than punishing them. Secondly, following on from this, biological positivism also believed that offenders were different from non-offenders, because they had particular biological characteristics which most 'normal' people did not have. Thirdly, as a result of these differences, biological positivists believed that offenders were different in this way because of problems in their biological or physical profile. Finally, biological positivist criminology was based around the idea of knowledge of the causes of crime which had to be gained through research, particularly experimentation. Unlike the abstract theorising used by classicism, only knowledge gained through direct experience was valid. Such research and experimentation also had to produce evidence of direct causal links between particular biological factors and the occurrence of crime. In building up a body of knowledge on the causes of crime in this way, experts (such as scientists and statisticians) could use their discretion not only to uncover the most effective ways to treat criminals so as to prevent them from offending again, but also to prevent crime from occurring in the first place by identifying and dealing with people who were predestined to be criminals before they had even begun to offend.

ASSESSMENT ADVICE

Essay and exam questions on positivism often take one of three forms: either asking you to compare the strengths and weaknesses of positivist explanations for crime to classicist explanations (see Chapter 5), asking you to consider whether positivist theories have any relevance to theories which attempt to explain crime today, or asking you to consider whether positivist explanations play any part in current criminal justice policy in England and Wales.

■ Sample question

Could you answer this question? Below is a typical essay question that could arise on this topic. Guidelines on answering the question are included at the end of this chapter. Another sample question and guidance on tackling it can be found on the companion website.

ESSAY QUESTION

'Biological positivism cannot explain why some people commit crime and other people do not in modern-day society.' Critically discuss this statement.

■ Biological positivist criminology

KEY DEFINITION: Biological positivist criminology

A set of ideas which claims to explain why crime is committed by identifying certain biological characteristics of or inside a person's body which are forcing that person to offend.

□□ REVISION NOTE

Positivism and classicism can appear together as part of a 'compare and contrast' exam question, so make sure that you revise the material on classicism in Chapter 5 alongside the material in this chapter. Also revise the Chapter 7 material alongside this chapter, since you may get an essay or exam question about positivism generally – while this chapter covers biological positivism, Chapter 7 covers psychological theories, many of which have been influenced by positivism.

Be critical

A really good essay or exam answer will avoid stating that positivism and classicism are completely different theories of crime, despite the apparent differences between them. You could show particularly acute analytical awareness by stating that both theories involve looking at particular influences on behaviour and assuming that those influences will lead to crime, and so do share some common ground.

While classicism argued that criminal justice punishment could influence a person in deciding whether or not to commit crime, positivism argued that biological or psychological factors could influence this decision. If this argument is accepted, the real difference between classicism and positivism is the decision about which factors are most likely to produce criminal behaviour, rather than completely different theoretical ideas about what causes crime.

✎ EXAM TIP

For extra marks in an exam on a question comparing positivism to classicism, emphasise the fact that although positivism and classicism have often been viewed as being completely opposite explanations for crime (because positivism tends to view crime as being beyond the offender's control, and classicism tends to view it as being a voluntary decision by the offender to offend), a more sophisticated view is that they do share common ground, because they both aim to discover which factors affect a person's decision to commit crime.

■ Key theorists and theories in biological positivist criminology

KEY THEORIST

Cesare Lombroso

Lombroso was a criminal anthropologist, who believed that criminals had not evolved to the same extent as non-criminals. As a result, criminals were 'primitive'. They had physical abnormalities which set them apart from ordinary people. The physical and biological characteristics which made them primitive also drove them to commit crime.

Lombroso's theory was derived from his observations of convicted offenders, both living and dead, in Sicily. He compared these offenders' physical features with those of people who had not been convicted, and also with those of people who had been diagnosed as mad, or 'lunatics':

■ He found that criminals tended to have such physical features as large jaws, excessive hairiness and abnormal teeth. It was these physical features, in his view, which drove criminals to offend.

■ This led Lombroso to develop four categories of criminal: born criminals who had the type of physical abnormalities discussed earlier, insane criminals who suffered from some kind of mental illness or abnormality, occasional criminals whose physical characteristics led them to take the opportunities to commit crime as they arose, and criminals of passion who offended due to an irresistible internal force.

■ As his work progressed, Lombroso took more social and environmental causes of crime into account, although he always retained the idea of primitive criminals predetermined to offend by their particular physical and biological characteristics to some extent.

Be critical

It is fairly easy to find criticisms of Lombroso when looking back on his ideas from a twenty-first-century standpoint – for example, Lombroso's use of physical and biological characteristics, and in particular his reliance upon physical features and illnesses such as epilepsy to explain crime can be seen as very over-simplistic. Although these are valid analytical points, try to be a little more inventive with your analysis on this issue – for example, by pointing out that Lombroso's research was mostly based on subjects in one particular place (Sicily), making it difficult to generalise his findings to other places.

KEY THEORIST

Enrico Ferri

Enrico Ferri rejected Lombroso's initial reliance on physical and biological characteristics to explain crime. Instead, Ferri placed much greater emphasis on the ability of offenders' social and environmental circumstances to cause crime.

However, Ferri was still a positivist. He retained positivism's use of scientific methods and observation to explain crime, and its belief that offenders were predetermined to offend by factors beyond their control. Since Ferri was a deterministic positivist, like Lombroso, his work can be criticised for assuming that anyone facing social or environmental problems in their lives will 'automatically' offend.

! Don't be tempted to . . .

Do not argue, in either essays or exams, that all positivist criminology uses internal and biological factors as the *only* means of explaining crime. As the discussion of Ferri's work above shows, some positivists have favoured environmental factors as explanations for crime alongside biological factors.

KEY THEORIST

Charles Goring

Goring's research was critical of Lombroso's theory that criminals had physical characteristics which set them apart from non-criminals. Goring compared 3,000 convicted criminals with a similarly sized group of non-criminals, such as students and soldiers. He found no physical or mental characteristics which were unique to offenders, although he did find that offenders tended to be physically smaller and less intelligent than others. As a result, he used hereditary factors as the main explanation for crime.

Be critical

Goring's research can be criticised for being outdated, as it is now almost a century old – but try to criticise his methodology as well, because positivists prided themselves on basing their theories on solid research evidence. You could argue, for example, that Goring did not examine all of the environmental factors which could have explained criminal behaviour instead of family traits, and failed to consider that some of his 'non-criminal' group might in fact have been unconvicted offenders – so in positivist terms, his theories were unsound.

EXAM TIP

As well as offering criticism of positivist assumptions about crime in general, try to show differences between different positivist thinkers in their approaches – such as the differences between Lombroso's early work and Ferri, for example, or Goring's criticism of Lombroso's assumptions about physical and mental differences between criminals and non-criminals.

KEY THEORIST

William Sheldon

Sheldon used body type as his main explanation for crime. Studying 200 boys who had been convicted as offenders, he identified three types of physique, each of which was linked to a particular personality type:

- endomorphic (fat, round build) linked with viscerotonic (relaxed, extrovert personality);

- mesomorphic (muscular build) linked with somotonic (dynamic, aggressive personality); and

- ectomorphic (thin build) linked with cerebrotonic (sensitive, introvert personality).

Sheldon found that the offenders in his sample were more likely to be mesomorphic and less likely to be ectomorphic. This study, similarly to other positivist work, has been criticised by a range of classicist and radical criminologists for over-simplistically assuming that having a particular body type drives people to commit crime.

KEY THEORIST

Sheldon and Eleanor Glueck

The Gluecks followed William Sheldon's use of body types as a way of explaining why people offend. However, they also used a range of environmental, psychological and emotional factors to explain crime, arguing that taking these factors into account would allow potential offenders to be identified at a very young age.

Although the determinism of positivism was still present in the Gluecks' work, and led to it being criticised as being too individualistic by classicist and radical criminologists, the use of a range of factors, some biological and some not, was an influence on more modern biological positivist theories.

KEY THEORY

Genetic criminology

One recent type of biological positivist criminology – **genetic criminology** – has, as its name suggests, centred on genetic explanations for crime. An example of this type of theory is the study of twins' criminal behaviour. Christiansen's work in Denmark found significantly higher rates of both twins having a criminal record for monozygotic twins (from the same fertilised egg and sharing the same genetic makeup) than for dizygotic twins (from different fertilised eggs and not sharing the same genetic makeup), suggesting that the genetic profile of twins increases their chances of offending.

Another example is the adoption study, where the offending records of adopted children are compared with their biological parents' offending and their adoptive parents' offending. Mednick's research, again in Denmark, found higher rates of offending among adopted children whose biological fathers had also been convicted criminals than among those whose adoptive fathers had offended. However, it is difficult to prove that environmental factors have not played any part in offending behaviour.

A third strand of genetic explanation has centred on chromosome abnormalities. A particular focus here has been whether men with an extra Y chromosome (XYY instead of the more common XY) are more violent than other men, but such small numbers of men are XYY, and so few XYY men are offenders, that no conclusive link has been found.

However, other work has shown a possible link between chromosomal abnormalities and attention deficit hyperactivity disorder (ADHD), which can in turn lead to antisocial or criminal behaviour. This suggests that biological positivism works best as a theory when teamed with more environmental explanations for crime.

KEY THEORY

Biochemical explanations

Biochemical criminology has identified and tested a range of biochemical factors within the body as possible explanations for crime. The first type has examined the central nervous system, to check whether offenders have abnormal signals being transmitted from the brain to the body. The second type of biochemical positivist research has examined what is known as the autonomic nervous system (ANS), which controls such key functions as heart rate and blood pressure.

If a child is punished when they behave badly, these ANS changes should be produced, leading the child to associate unpleasant feelings such as an increased heart rate with antisocial behaviour, and avoid such behaviour in the future:

- The faster a person's ANS responds to antisocial behaviour, and the faster the ANS recovers from fear, the less likely they are to offend.

- On the other hand, if a person's ANS is slow to recover, they are less likely to associate committing crime with feeling unpleasant, and therefore more likely to commit crime, according to Mednick's research.

- Thirdly, research has been centred on more minor brain abnormalities, such as attention deficit hyperactivity disorder (ADHD). ADHD has been linked with low IQs and family history of offending, and in turn with antisocial or criminal behaviour, in the research of David Farrington and others.

- The fourth type of biochemical positivist research which could be discussed in essay or exam answers focuses on neurotransmitters, or chemicals which allow information to be processed by the brain. Research has found links between low levels of one particular neurotransmitter which suppresses aggression – serotonin – and antisocial or criminal behaviour.

- Fifthly, research has also focused upon the possible effects of levels of hormones in the body upon criminal behaviour. In particular, the links between high levels of the hormone testosterone and aggressive criminal behaviour have been investigated.

✎ EXAM TIP

Although biological positivist research and theorising has clearly developed and changed since Lombroso's 'primitive criminal' theory, make the case for similarities between older and more modern work, as well as for a more rounded exam answer. The main general link between them is the search for one 'X factor' which will predict crime every time it occurs, or at least most of the time it occurs, in a particular person. There are also more specific links, such as the biochemical research into the effects of epileptic seizures, which also formed part of Lombroso's early theories.

Be critical

There are two lines of argument which, if you corroborate your analysis with reliable evidence, will provide an effective source of critical analysis of biochemical criminology. Consider the argument that biochemical theories overlook possible alternative social or environmental explanations for crime. For example, further research on the links between ANS and criminal behaviour has suggested that the relationship between slow-recovering ANS and crime only applies to people who have a low social or economic status – leading to criticisms that the effects of ANS only lead to offending when someone also experiences a deprived or problematic environment, when growing up for example.

Research has found difficulty in proving a definitive link between biochemical factors and crime – the kind of 'black and white' explanation for crime which biological positivism has traditionally looked for. For example, you could point out that researchers have found it difficult to determine whether high testosterone causes aggression, or vice versa; and that testosterone levels can increase temporarily in a person, even if they are normal for most of the time.

✎ EXAM TIP

To give more breadth to an essay or exam question about biological positivism, you could include discussion of possible influences on crime which are triggered by external or environmental factors, but which have biological or other internal effects on a person – such as a harmful intake of alcohol, drugs or certain unhealthy types of food.

Make your answer stand out

An important recent debate involving biological positivist criminology relates to the work of Wilson and Herrnstein (1985) and Currie (1991), who rejects Wilson and Herrnstein's ideas. This debate is important because it provides an excellent example of how biological positivist ideas can influence modern criminology, how its values can be blended with those from other criminological theories such as classicism, and how theories which focus more on socio-economic explanations for crime criticise biological positivist ideas.

■ Biological positivist criminology's influences on criminal justice policy

This section deals briefly with how a criminal justice system based around biological positivism might look.

One concern which has traditionally been raised with biological positivism is that, if used in practice (e.g. to identify one or more genes which led to criminal behaviour), it could lead to the removal of identified criminals from society to prevent further offending – through detention, the death penalty or even sterilisation to prevent the passing on of biological 'criminal genes' to future generations.

The extremism of the scenarios above has normally deterred criminal justice from using these policies. Despite this, it has commonly been argued, by David Garland and others, that British criminology was heavily influenced by biological positivism in the first half of the twentieth century, and that this influence resulted in a focus on treatment and rehabilitation for offenders in the criminal justice system, rather than the classicist emphasis on punishment and deterrence.

 Make your answer stand out

Garland (1985) argues that biological positivism was not the only influence on British criminology and criminal justice in the first half of the twentieth century. Use his work to support critical analysis of the influence of biological positivism in criminal justice practice.

As shown above, a large amount of modern biological positivist research has recognised that biology can only be used to explain crime when considered together with more social and environmental reasons. Modern research has also struggled to identify a direct causal link between biological factors and crime which is not affected by any other non-biological influences, as positivism has traditionally demanded.

These factors have contributed to a decline in the influence of biological positivism as a standalone explanation for crime. Nonetheless, the progress of hybrid biological and social research and theories shows that biological positivism continues to have influence in criminology generally – recent campaigns to improve prisoners' diets as a means of reducing reoffending is just one example of its continuing role.

Positivism's commitment to practical research, such as observation, as the main way of gathering knowledge about crime ensures that it has influenced all of the other criminological theories that have emerged since the late nineteenth century, in methodological terms.

■ Putting it all together

Answer guidelines

See the essay question at the start of the chapter.

Approaching the question

This question is asking you about what influence (if any) biological positivism has on modern-day explanations for crime. The question covers all uses of biological positivism currently, so after showing your knowledge of what biological positivism stood for in the past, you would want to make sure that you considered not only theories which incorporate biological positivism, but also policies which have incorporated and could incorporate it.

Important points to include

- Introduction mapping out the overall structure of the essay in brief.
- Statement of the key principles of positivism in general.
- Statement of the key principles of biological positivism in particular, and a brief overview of key writers such as Lombroso and their beliefs.
- The focus of the essay should be on modern-day biological positivist research and its strengths and weaknesses. You should identify such categories of research as genetic studies and biochemical studies – and broaden out the discussion with evidence of the links between crime and drugs, alcohol and poor diet, all of which

can influence biological factors. Remember to identify the problems with each type of research as well as what it claims to prove – especially the increasing reliance upon social and environmental factors to explain crime in conjunction with biological factors.

- Critical consideration of how biological positivism influences criminal justice policy and practice.
- Conclusions summarising the essay's arguments and explaining the essay's position on biological positivism's current influence on criminology.

 Make your answer stand out

- Emphasise the diversity in ideas within biological positivism – for example comparing Lombroso with Sheldon or the Gluecks' work.
- Emphasise the great influence that biological positivism has had on other criminological theories, in terms of its emphasis on primary research and observation as a way of gaining knowledge about crime.
- Emphasise the common ground between biological positivism and classicism, in terms of looking for factors which influence criminal behaviour. You could use Wilson and Herrnstein's work as an example of how this could work.

READ TO IMPRESS

Currie, E. (1991) 'The Politics of Crime: The American Experience', in Stenson, K. and Cowell, D. (eds), *The Politics of Crime Control* London: Sage.

Garland, D. (1985) *Punishment and Welfare,* Aldershot: Gower.

Gottfredson, M.R. and Hirschi, T. (eds.) (1987) *Positive Criminology,* London: Sage.

Pick, D. (1993) *Faces of Degeneration: A European Disorder, c.1848–c.1918,* Chapter 5, Cambridge: Cambridge University Press.

Taylor, I., Walton, P. and Young, J. (1973) *The New Criminology,* Chapter 1, London: Routledge and Kegan Paul.

Wilson, J.Q. and Herrnstein, R. (1985) *Crime and Human Nature,* New York: Simon and Schuster.

www.pearsoned.co.uk/lawexpress

 Go online to access more revision support, including quizzes to test your knowledge, sample questions with answer guidelines, podcasts you can download, and more!

Psychological explanations of crime

7

Revision checklist

Essential points you should know:

☐ The main types of psychological research which can be used as criminological explanations, and their respective strengths and weaknesses

☐ The extent to which criminal personality theories are capable of explaining different types of criminal behaviour

☐ How theories which focus on emotions attempt to explain crime

☐ The extent to which these psychological explanations for crime influence criminal justice policy

■Topic map

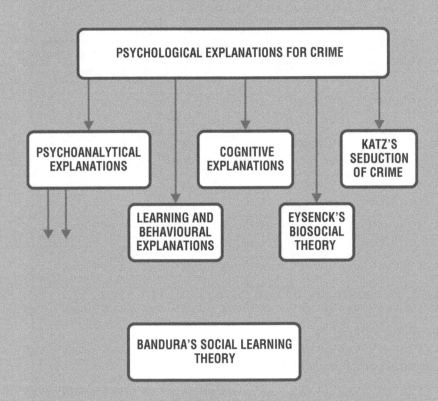

■ Introduction

Psychological explanations have become increasingly high-profile in media images of the causes of crime in the past 20 years.

These images have influenced the common public perception that criminals are somehow 'different' or 'abnormal' compared to the rest of society. Yet psychology's focus on internal, individual causes of crime has meant that it has often had little in common with criminologists who look for the causes of crime in social conditions such as poverty and inequality. This chapter will guide you through the key thinkers and theories within the psychological discipline, as well as examining how close psychology's relationship with criminology has been.

ASSESSMENT ADVICE

Questions relating to psychological explanations for crime will tend to focus on the extent to which psychological theories focus on internal factors within the individual and so ignore possible external causes of crime. They may also ask you to discuss the impact which psychology has had on criminology, either in terms of theory, criminal justice practice, or both.

■ Sample question

Could you answer this question? Below is a typical essay question that could arise on this topic. Guidelines on answering the question are included at the end of this chapter. Another sample question and guidance on tackling it can be found on the companion website.

ESSAY QUESTION

'Psychological theories focus too much on internal, brain-related causes of crime and not enough on external causes, and as a result they have only ever had a limited impact on understandings of why crime is committed, in both theory and practice.' Critically discuss this statement.

■ Psychological explanations

> **KEY DEFINITION: Psychological criminology**
>
> A set of theories which focus on the personality, learning processes, emotions and other brain-related activities within an individual's mind as explanations for why crime is committed.

> **KEY THEORY**
>
> *Psychoanalytical theories of crime*
>
> **Psychoanalytical theories** are derived from the work of Sigmund Freud. Freud argued that violent or aggressive acts are the result of conflict between the different elements of the conscious and subconscious mind, and more specifically traumatic events experienced during early childhood.

For Freud, the mind was divided into three parts:

- the subconscious id, which controls basic and instinctual behaviour, and whose aim is to seek pleasurable and satisfying experiences at all costs;

- the mostly conscious super-ego, which acts as a source of guilt and conscience, and as a moral and ethical regulator on behaviour; and

- the mostly conscious ego, which balances the needs of the id and super-ego in line with what is realistic in terms of behaviour, while trying to find ways to give the id what it wants.

Freud therefore concluded that deviant behaviour was the result of the moral super-ego not being fully developed, giving the id too much power in a person's mind.

> **✎ EXAM TIP**
>
> Be careful not to quote Freud directly too much when discussing psychoanalytical approaches to crime. Freud himself actually wrote very little about crime, instead preferring to discuss 'deviant behaviour' (which may or may not be legally defined as a crime). In an exam, you should therefore acknowledge Freud's influence on psychoanalytical explanations of crime, but discuss in more detail those who were influenced by him and focused more directly on crime.

Freud's followers did research which argued that the crime which resulted from a poorly developed super-ego was the result of poor parenting – either in terms of parents neglecting or spoiling their children. John Bowlby focused on maternal deprivation in the early years of life, arguing that the more a child was either rejected or physically separated from its mother, the more crime that child would commit later on in life.

Be critical

The criticisms of psychoanalytical theories, especially Bowlby's work, have been used over a long period of time, so you would be expected to refer to them in your analysis during essay and exam answers. For example, you could argue that they cannot be fully empirically tested by research, because they centre on the unconscious desires within a person's mind as the cause of crime, and their success may also depend largely upon the skill and judgment of an individual psychoanalyst in analysing the causes of crime – again something which is hard to measure in research terms, and therefore against the principles of positivist theory.

📖 REVISION NOTE

The focus of psychoanalysis on innate, primeval urges as the cause of crime is very similar to the biological positivist criminologists' portrayal of criminals as not fully developed and primitive due to forces beyond their control. Therefore, refer back to the discussion of the work of biological positivists in Chapter 6 when revising this topic.

KEY THEORY

Learning and behavioural theories

Learning theories try to explain how crime occurs as a result of criminal behaviour being learned from others through interaction between individuals and the world around them. Various types of learning theory differ primarily in terms of the relative importance of the social or environmental factor(s) which influence behaviour, and of individual freedom of choice following this influence, as causes of criminal behaviour.

Edwin Sutherland's differential association theory, whereby criminal behaviour is learned from associating with those who already commit crime where there are more unfavourable (criminal) definitions of behaviour in a person's life than favourable (non-criminal) ones, was the first learning theory which tried to bring together psychological and criminological perspectives on why crime occurs, although psychologists largely overlooked the social dimension of Sutherland's work, preferring to focus more on individual behaviour as the key explanation for crime.

📖 **REVISION NOTE**

Sutherland's differential association theory is discussed in more detail in Chapter 8, so revise the material on his work there alongside the material in this chapter.

Another variant of learning theory which has been applied to criminology is behaviourist theory, based on the work of B.F. Skinner, who looked at how environmental conditions trigger off individual behaviour, which then produces consequences which are either desirable (because they are reinforced) or undesirable (because they are punished) to the individual. This theory looks to the balance between the rewards and drawbacks of committing crime for each individual to explain why and how crime happens.

✎ **EXAM TIP**

Show a deeper understanding of Jeffrey's hybrid learning theory by questioning the extent to which the theory really considers social factors which could, for example, explain crime, such as poverty and abuse of social power, as deeply as criminologists have done.

C.R. Jeffrey was the first psychologist to apply Skinner's ideas specifically to crime, by merging them with Sutherland's differential association theory. Jeffrey argued that crime was the result of both social and cultural environments and the results of crime for the individual (in terms of how criminal behaviour was reinforced).

Jeffrey's theory of differential reinforcement has been developed further by Ron Akers, who has identified four aspects of how differential reinforcement can lead to crime, explaining why individual people behave differently in criminal terms when faced with similar environmental triggers:

- Differential association, or how frequently and intensively someone associates with people who commit crime, either physically or through media such as the Internet.

- Social definitions of behaviour which could lead to how an individual attaches meanings to their own behaviour.

- Differential reinforcement, whereby the individual behaves according to the actual or anticipated consequences of behaviour, and crime is either reinforced or not reinforced.

- Imitation, where an individual decides whether or not to imitate others' criminal behaviour based what kind of person is being observed, the type of behaviour which is observed, and the consequences of that behaviour for others.

Make your answer stand out

Read Akers (1998) for a recent and comprehensive application of social learning theory (more specifically differential reinforcement theory) to issues relating to why crime occurs, and critically discuss the extent to which this theory can be described as psychological positivism due to its social influences.

Be critical

You should consider the extent to which the theories of behaviourist psychologists such as Skinner and Jeffrey could be argued to have swapped one type of positivism for another. You should assess the validity of the argument, for example that their theories overcame the difficulties of measuring the psychoanalytical causes of crime, but do not escape from the problem of determinism: the idea that people are driven to act in certain ways (e.g. committing crime) under certain conditions.

Skinner was arguing that criminal behaviour was an automatic response to certain environmental triggers, without any freedom of choice on the part of the offender – a theory which unrealistically ignores any freedom of choice over whether or not to commit crime on the part of the individual offender.

There are questions over Skinner's and Sutherland's usage of the concept of balances to explain crime, in terms of crime occurring if there are more reinforcements of, or associations with, criminal behaviour than not.

Neither theorist fully explained how these balances or associations could be measured, or how many reinforcements or associations would be required before crime would be committed. Behaviourist theories' focus on determinism and individual criminal behaviour rather than the external causes of that behaviour have left them open to sustained criticism from radical criminologists such as those discussed in Chapter 9.

KEY THEORIST

Albert Bandura

Bandura's work is so significant because he developed cognitive social learning theory, merging external factor-focused behaviourism of Skinner's work with more internally focused aspects of cognitive psychology to focus on three aspects of why crime might occur:

- learning things and behaviour;
- the social context of learning from other people; and
- cognition, or processes of the brain such as understanding and perception, which are unique to human beings.

Bandura argued that people learned behaviour through observing the behaviour of others. Then, once behaviour had been learned, it could be reinforced (through the environment generally, observation or pleasure gained by the individual from their own actions) or punished by social and external factors. It was internal cognitive processes, though, such as thoughts and attitudes, which processed and mediated the effects of external stimuli on individual behaviour, and thereby determined what effects those external stimuli would have on a person's actions.

✎ EXAM TIP

Show detailed knowledge of Bandura's 'Bobo doll' experiment on how children learn and imitate aggressive behaviour from observing situations (on film) where aggressive behaviour was rewarded. For example, mention that Bandura used an experimental research design to carry out his research: some of the children were shown a film without aggressive content or a film where aggressive behaviour was shown, but was punished rather than rewarded. It was this design which gave Bandura more confidence in saying that it was watching rewarded aggressive behaviour on film which caused the children to behave violently themselves.

📖 REVISION NOTE

Refer back to the discussion of Bandura's work in the context of the impact of media images on criminal behaviour in Chapter 4 when thinking about the importance of his research.

Be critical

Again keeping positivist theoretical principles in mind, you can criticise Bandura's work in terms of the question marks over the quality of the research on which he based his social learning theory. For example, you could argue in an essay or exam answer that the Bobo doll experiment is ethically controversial, and that the children in the study were being trained to behave aggressively and criminally just to prove a theoretical point.

Also, it is difficult to prove conclusively that watching the film caused the children's violence – other internal or external factors might have been just as influential on their behaviour as the film was. This returns us to the traditional psychological problem of proving that one thing directly causes another, as opposed to just having an influence upon it.

KEY THEORIST

Hans Eysenck

Eysenck's work focused on particular, genetically inherited and biologically centred personality characteristics, and how the varying development of these characteristics shaped responses to external factors, predisposing some people to commit crime through their inability to be conditioned to behave well through socialisation. He described his theory as biosocial – influenced by biology and genetics, but taking into account external stimuli and individual differences as well.

Eysenck measured people's personalities according to how they scored on three different scales – the higher a person's combined score, the less able they were to be conditioned in early life through socialisation, and the more likely they were to commit crime:

- extroversion (E – outgoing, cheerful, expressive);

- neuroticism (N – emotionally unstable, anxious, moody); and

- psychoticism (P – aggressive, selfish, sociopathic).

As a result of these scales of personality measurement, Eysenck claimed to be able to identify accurately those who were most likely to commit crime, since most people scored somewhere in the middle of each scale, and so only an easily identifiable minority would commit the majority of crime. Eysenck also claimed that different types of crime could be matched to different types of criminal personality, in terms of different combinations of the E, N and P scores.

 Make your answer stand out

Use Eysenck and Gudjonsson (1989) as an accessible introduction to Eysenck's often complex theoretical ideas, and to how those ideas can be used in criminal justice practice.

Be critical

Use the work of critical criminologists, such as Taylor, Walton and Young in their book *The New Criminology,* to point out the flaws in Eysenck's work. Radical criminologists attacked Eysenck for relying on biological determinism and genetic inheritance to explain criminality.

You could also criticise Eysenck for discounting the role of individual free will in committing crime (an argument which you could use the work of both criminologists and psychologists such as Akers in support of), for overlooking social and political causes of crime, and for ignoring the fact that crime is a social construction. The point of these analytical approaches should be that it is meaningless to state, as Eysenck did, that criminals and non-criminals are separate and distinct social groups.

Others have criticised the empirical basis of Eysenck's research:

■ All three of his personality traits have been extensively researched by psychologists, and although relationships have been generally found between high psychoticism and neuroticism levels and criminal behaviour, little evidence has been found of a link between high extroversion levels and crime. This lack of data makes Eysenck's theory less convincing.

■ As with other psychological explanations of crime, it is also difficult to prove conclusively that personality type and its effect upon childhood socialisation is the definitive and universal cause of crime, as opposed to being linked to crime in some cases.

KEY THEORY

Cognitive theories

Drawing on the work of the psychologist Jean Piaget, who focused on the development of the ability to use moral reasoning to guide behaviour as a person goes through life, **cognitive theories** focus upon the ways in which a person thinks and solves problems as an explanation for crime, arguing that criminals reason cognitively and make choices in different ways to non-criminals.

Yochelson and Samenow (1976) claimed to have identified the thinking patterns and errors that distinguished criminals from non-criminals. They argued that all criminals shared these wrongful cognitive patterns in common. In total Yochelson and Samenow identified a range of these cognitive errors, which they split into three different categories:

■ character traits, such as feelings of worthlessness;

■ automatic thinking errors, such as a failure to empathise with others; and

■ errors associated with criminal acts, such as super-optimism.

As a result, Yochelson and Samenow argued not only that criminals could be distinguished from non-criminals by their thought processes, but also that criminality was caused by these faulty thought processes, not by a person's environment or social situation.

Be critical

You should be able to identify several distinct problems with the approach of cognitive theories to explaining crime, rather just isolating one issue. Firstly, you should point out that cognitivists' assertion that all criminals share the same thought processes is problematic given the wide range of criminal behaviours which exist – and, on a related issue, given the changing nature of crime and the fact that most crime goes unreported, it is almost impossible to state that criminals and non-criminals can be easily distinguished.

Another issue is the narrow focus of the theory's explanation on internal, psychological explanations for crime – there is no room for social or biological explanations for crime in this theory.

✎ EXAM TIP

Show knowledge of the methodological base underpinning Yochelson and Samenow's study when discussing their work – in fact their findings were based entirely upon interviews with only 240 offenders, all of whom were criminally insane and in prison.

KEY THEORIST

Jack Katz

Katz's explanation of crime as an activity which can give emotional and sensual pleasure to those who commit it focuses on the psychological emotions and thought processes which occur before and after a crime is committed. In Katz's view, the seductions of particular types of crime can explain why people who fit the profile of sociological, psychological or biological theories of crime do not commit crime in practice, or why people suddenly switch from a rational choice not to offend to a compulsion to offend in a few seconds.

Katz explains a wide range of criminal behaviour, from theft and robbery through to homicide, through the seductive pleasure that offenders gain from committing these acts. Katz identifies a range of emotions which can provide the seductive 'compulsion trigger' to commit crime, such as:

- thrill-seeking and excitement, which could explain apparently pointless but risky acts such as vandalism;

- revenge, which could explain hate crime as a response to actual or perceived injustices at the hands of another social or ethnic group: and

- humiliation and damage to self-esteem, which could, for example, explain homicides within relationships where the killer was provoked by the victim's infidelity

Make your answer stand out

Katz's book *Seductions of Crime* (1988) is the classic statement of his ideas on crime as an emotionally thrilling and pleasurable experience.

! Don't be tempted to . . .

Don't fall into the trap of arguing that Katz dismisses other psychological and social explanations of crime in developing his own theory. Katz does not deny that these theories play a background role in explaining crime. Rather, he tries to complement them by revealing the psychological 'foreground' of the immediate circumstances of offending.

Be critical

Carefully read the work of those who criticise Katz's theories (Jock Young in particular), and consider whether Katz pays too much attention to the psychological immediacy of offending, and not enough attention to the social and structural context of life, which shapes the way that people experience opportunities for crime.

Katz has also been criticised for over-romanticising offending. His work has a tendency to overlook the harm caused by 'seductive' behaviours such as robbery and murder.

■ Psychology's influences on criminal justice policy

Psychology and criminology may have had long-standing differences in terms of academic debates, but that has not prevented psychology from having a series of key influences on criminal justice policy:

■ In police work, psychology is used to select recruits and improve the quality of their decision-making, and to improve interviewing and interrogation techniques, as well as to build offender profiles to help with explaining the type of person who has committed a particular crime, and why.

■ Psychology also plays a range of roles in the courtroom. For example, psychologists regularly assess defendants with mental disorders, in order to give evidence to the court on whether a defendant is fit to stand trial, or whether a defendant is entitled to use a defence to reduce the seriousness of the charges against them on the grounds of their disorder. Psychology has also been used to understand how witnesses to crime process what they see, how they remember it and how well they can recall it when giving evidence, as well as to understand how (and how well) juries make a decision on whether someone is guilty or not guilty.

■ Finally, psychologically influenced intervention techniques have been extensively used in England and Wales in the past 20 years as part of punishment programmes run by probation and prison officers, particularly in the form of cognitive-behavioural pro-grammes which aim to change the ways in which offenders think about crime, about themselves, and about other people. These programmes have worked well in some cases, but have also been criticised for marginalising other forms of intervention, and for being evaluated in a very narrow and restricted way in terms of measuring their success.

 Make your answer stand out

The work of David Canter (e.g. Canter and Alison, 2000) for an example of how psy-chological offender profiling can be used in criminal justice practice, but be critical with this source – for example, question the risk of applying previous knowledge about offender's psychological profiles in terms of potential miscarriages of justice, if innocent people who match those profiles are wrongly convicted.

■ Putting it all together

Answer guidelines

See the essay question at the start of the chapter.

Approaching the question

This question is in three parts. The first part asks you to assess the extent to which psychological theories of crime focus on internal factors at the expense of social and environmental factors. The second part then asks you to assess the extent of

▶

psychology's influence on criminal justice policy. The third part joins the previous two together, because it asks you to assess the strength of the link between the internal focus and the limited influence.

Important points to include

- Introduction briefly showing awareness of the basic principles of psychological explanations of crime, and mapping out the rest of the essay.

- Critical discussion of the major psychological theories which try to explain why crime occurs – for example, for example, psychoanalytical, learning and behavioural, Eysenck's biosocial and cognitive – and the extent to which they overemphasise internal causes of crime and overlook external and social causes.

- Critical discussion of the ways in which psychology has influenced criminal justice policy, in terms of police, courtroom and punishment practice, and an overall assessment of how much these practices have influenced criminal justice in general compared with practice not influenced by psychology.

- In the light of the results of discussion in the two previous areas, assessment of how closely related psychology's theoretical focus and the extent of its influence on criminology are.

- Conclusion summarising the key points made during the essay.

 Make your answer stand out

- Critically analyse the claims of some psychological theories that they take social factors into account when explaining crime – for example, Eysenck's biosocial theory claims to do this, but was heavily criticised by critical criminologists for not investigating these issues in enough depth.

- Always- pay attention to, and critique, the evidence used as the base for different psychological theories – for example, Yochelson and Samenow's general theory of criminal cognition was based on a small selective sample of offenders.

- Where possible, use research evidence to assess how valuable psychology is to criminal justice in practice – for example, how much have police interrogation techniques actually improved as a direct result of the application of psychological knowledge?

READ TO IMPRESS

Akers, R. (1998) *Social Learning and Social Structure: A general theory of crime and deviance,* Boston, MA: Northeastern University Press.

Bandura, A. (1977) *Social Learning Theory,* New York: Prentice Hall.

Bowlby, J. (1973) [*Attachment and Loss, Vol. 2:*] *Separation: Anxiety and anger,* London: Hogarth Press.

Canter, D. and Alison, L. (2000) *Profiling Property Crimes,* Aldershot: Ashgate.

Eysenck, H. and Gudjonsson, G. (1989) *The Causes and Cures of Criminality,* New York: Plenum Press.

Katz, J. (1988) *Seductions of Crime,* New York: Basic Books.

Yochelson, S. and Samenow, S. (1976) *The Criminal Personality,* New York: Jason Aronson.

www.pearsoned.co.uk/lawexpress

 Go online to access more revision support, including quizzes to test your knowledge, sample questions with answer guidelines, podcasts you can download, and more!

Sociological explanations of crime

8

Revision checklist

Essential points you should know:

- [ ] The Chicago School theory of geographical environment as a cause of crime
- [ ] Edwin Sutherland's theory of differential association, and how mixing with criminals allows people to learn how to commit crime
- [ ] The strain and subcultural theories of Merton, Cohen, and Cloward and Ohlin
- [ ] The labelling theory of Lemert and Becker

▌Topic map

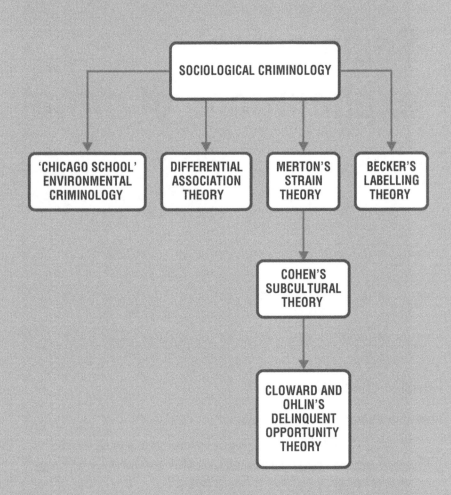

■ Introduction

Throughout the mid-twentieth century, criminologists moved away from explaining crime purely in terms of biological or psychological problems within each individual offender.

Instead, the focus began to move onto conditions in society – poverty, unemployment and the distribution of wealth, for example – and how they might be able to explain why crime occurs. From these roots, a wide range of criminological theories based around societal and environmental factors were developed by the theorists discussed in this chapter.

ASSESSMENT ADVICE

Apart from asking you to compare the strengths and weaknesses of a particular theory in terms of its ability to explain crime, essay and exam questions may also ask you to assess the extent to which sociological criminological theories broke away from the positivistic criminologies discussed in Chapters 6 and 7.

■ Sample question

Could you answer this question? Below is a typical essay question that could arise on this topic. Guidelines on answering the question are included at the end of this chapter. Another sample question and guidance on tackling it can be found on the companion website.

ESSAY QUESTION

'No sociologically based theory of crime has succeeded in breaking away completely from the flawed determinism of the positivistic approach to explaining crime.' Critically discuss this statement.

■ Key theorists and theories in sociological criminology

KEY DEFINITION: Sociological criminology

A set of theoretical explanations for why crime occurs which focus on conditions in society and geographical environment as the primary explanation for why individuals commit crime, rather than individual, biological or psychological factors within a particular individual.

> ✎ **EXAM TIP**
>
> For extra marks in an exam on a question concerning one or more sociological or envi-ronmental theories of crime, mention the idea that, although many of these theories try to move away from deterministic individual positivism, they still study the ways in which social and environmental factors *influence* the internal thought processes of individual offenders, resulting in the commission of crime. So, even theories which appear to be driven by societal causes of crime still have to (or at least should) take what occurs in the minds of offenders into account.

> **KEY THEORISTS**
>
> *The Chicago School*
>
> The Chicago School argued that it was where a person lived which determined whether or not they would commit crime. Shaw and McKay divided Chicago into different geographical zones, starting with the central business district, then the inner city area known as the 'zone of transition', and moving outwards through increasingly affluent residential areas. Despite this constant change in population as immigrants became more wealthy and moved further away from the city, crime rates remained constant in the zone of transition, and declined steadily the further away people lived from the city centre.

The Chicago School writers used official criminal statistics on arrest rates and where offenders lived to map out rates of offending in different areas of the city of Chicago. The explanation given by the Chicago School for high urban crime rates was social disorganisation – the chaotic conditions of the zone of transition, where there was little respect for the law. In areas close to the centre of the city, the population was constantly changing due to successive waves of new immigrants, living conditions tended to be poor and social control over individuals' behaviour was weak. In the zone of transition, crime was a normal, everyday occurrence, and was passed onto new arrivals through the process of cultural transmission. With this research, the Chicago School pioneered a new kind of **environmental criminology.**

> ✎ **EXAM TIP**
>
> When answering an exam question on environmental criminology, you should acknowl-edge the influence which this type of theory has had over criminal justice policy, both in the Chicago School's own time, when it inspired various social projects designed to improve inner-city living conditions, and more recently, in the sense that particular envi-ronments are still linked with crime – when politicians talk about geographical 'crime hot spots' where crime is seen as being a particularly serious problem, for example.

Revise the material on classicist criminology in Chapter 5 alongside the Chicago School's environmental criminology, because more modern criminologists (such as Brantingham and Brantingham and Felson) have pointed to the influence of environmental factors on opportunities for offenders to make the rational choice to commit crime. One example of this would be evidence of increased crime rates in urban areas with poor street lighting.

Be critical

You could critique the Chicago School's ideas by considering the limitations of their positivist standpoint. Firstly, consider the extent to which their theories' failure to acknowledge the limitations of official crime statistics (in the sense that they did not include crime which is not recorded by the police) damages the ability of the theory to explain crime. You could argue that any picture of crime based on data from police statistics is likely to be distorted, since it will inevitably overemphasise street crime and under-represent types of crime which tend to be reported less frequently, such as sexual crimes, or corporate and organised crime.

Environmental criminology also ignored other possible explanations for crime, such as the rational choice and opportunity theories used by classicism (see chapter 5). Lastly, the Chicago School theories were based entirely on Chicago itself. Research done elsewhere (e.g. in the UK) has shown that other cities cannot be neatly divided into concentric social zones, as the Chicago School theorists claimed to be able to do with their own city. This clearly limits the extent to which the theory can explain crime outside Chicago.

! Don't be tempted to . . .

Be careful about overstating the differences between the Chicago School's environmental theory of crime and earlier biological positivism. Although the Chicago School rejected biological positivism's claim that certain biological or physiological characteristics drive a person to offend, they did maintain the view that certain environmental conditions (e.g. living in the zone of transition) forced a person to offend. Therefore, the criticism of biological positivism's deterministic approach can be applied to the Chicago School's theories as well.

Sutherland and differential association theory

Sutherland argued that people learn about techniques of committing crime through inter-actions with friends, family and others whom they like and respect. As a result of these interactions, people pick up different motives, attitudes, beliefs and definitions which are either in favour of or against committing crime. When an individual experiences more definitions and beliefs which are in favour of breaking the law than are against breaking the law (through being surrounded by others who break the law), then they are more likely to commit crime themselves. Therefore, '**differential association**' with others who commit crime is the main explanation for crime, in Sutherland's view.

Sutherland was particularly interested in the process of the cultural transmission of crimi-nal behaviour from one person to another. Like the Chicago School, he believed that an individual's environment, and their social interactions with other people, can influence that individual's chances of offending. However, Sutherland saw the transmission of criminal behaviour on a more individual, psychological level than the Chicago School did. He argued that differential association leading to criminal behaviour was especially likely if one or more of the following situations applied:

- when such association happens early in a person's life;
- when it occurs intensively;
- when it occurs frequently; and
- when it occurs over a long period of time.

When discussing differential association, note its links to psychological theories of crime through its emphasis on processes of individuals learning about crime – a factor which links back to more positivistic psychological theories of crime.

When revising Sutherland's differential association theory, refer back to his definition of crime as the breach of social norms, discussed in Chapter 1. It was this focus on socially harmful activities, which were not necessarily defined legally as crimes, which led Sutherland to attempt to develop a criminological theory which was capable of explaining both types of criminal behaviour, in the form of differential association.

Be critical

The easiest way to incorporate critical analysis of Sutherland's theory into an essay or exam answer is by accusing the theory of being too vague in defining how differential association actually works. As evidence for this claim, you could point out that no definitive list of favourable and unfavourable crime definitions was ever provided as part of the theory, and so no attempt was ever made to find out whether offenders really do have more favourable definitions than unfavourable ones, or to find out how many more favourable definitions than unfavourable ones were needed before crime would be committed.

Differential association also fails to explain how crime originally began, if all criminal behaviour is learned from someone else, and how newly defined crimes would be learned. It could therefore be argued that, although differential association theory sounds like a convincing explanation for crime in principle, it cannot be tested fully by research in practice.

 Make your answer stand out

For a really comprehensive discussion of differential association theory, read and discuss Sutherland's (1949) influential study of white-collar crime. Also, discuss the historical and social context in which the study was produced: the fact that an uncensored edition of the book (naming all of the businesses whom Sutherland found guilty of criminal activity) was not published until 1983, long after Sutherland's death, tells us a lot about the ability of the powerful to mask or downplay their own criminal activity.

KEY THEORY

Durkheim, Merton, anomie and strain theory

Émile Durkheim argued that crime was not only a normal part of everyday life, but also that it was useful to society, because its existence helped to define the limits of what was considered to be morally acceptable behaviour. This in turn enabled a society to remain unified in terms of which behaviour was allowed, and which was not, through allowing morals (and the law) to evolve as societal beliefs changed. Once a society's collective beliefs on acceptable behaviour came under stress, or broke down completely, the result was anomie, or law-breaking.

Robert Merton's **strain theory** argued that crime occurred when social conditions placed strain on individuals. Merton thought that crime would occur when people accepted the goals set by society (e.g. financial success), but could not achieve those goals because of society blocking their opportunities to succeed – they lacked the means to achieve their goals.

Merton believed that the poorest in society were therefore under the most 'strain', and therefore were most likely to commit crime as an illegal way of achieving success. His argument was backed up by FBI statistics which showed that young, poor males were most likely to commit property crime. Merton developed his strain theory further by classifying society into five different groups, depending on how people reacted to the strain which they were put under – in other words, whether or not group members accepted society's goals, and whether or not they had the opportunities to achieve those goals through legal means. He named these groups as follows:

- conformity;

- innovation;

- ritualism;

- retreatism; and

- rebellion.

The innovation and ritualism types were the clearest examples of strain, because in each case there was inconsistency between goals and means: one was accepted and one was rejected in each case. The theory provided a key explanation for why societies continue to experience crime as a social problem, even when they become wealthier.

Be critical

Since strain theory is a form of sociological positivism, you can use similar criticisms here to ones which could be used for biological positivism – for example, you could point to strain theory's failure to account for the experiences of women (since the statistics used to test the theory related only to young male offenders), and its use of official statistics, which do not and cannot include every crime which is committed.

Strain theory could also be criticised for being over-simplistic, for several reasons:

- not everyone in society shares the same goals (particularly in relation to financial success);

- not every society has the kind of culture which is focused on financial success as an attainment goal, as the USA had in Merton's time;

- not all crimes are committed to make money; and

- strain theory ignores the ways in which values and beliefs relating to crime are developed in groups.

✎ EXAM TIP

Add depth to an essay or exam answer about strain theory by showing knowledge of the social context in which it was developed. Merton was developing his ideas during the aftermath of the Great Depression in 1930s' America, when it was a commonly held view in society that financial wealth could be achieved by anyone who was willing to work hard enough. In practice, however, millions of people at that time were living in extreme poverty, because they did not have the opportunities to succeed. You could question whether Merton's theory is therefore so closely tied in with its social context that it could not work to explain crime in other societies and at other times in history.

 Make your answer stand out

Use the work of Agnew (1992) to examine how a more modern-day strain theory, which tests out Merton's ideas using empirical research and focuses more on individual personality characteristics, meets the criticisms of Merton's ideas.

KEY THEORIST

Cohen's subcultural theory

Albert Cohen's **subcultural theory** disagreed with Merton about crime always having the goal of financial gain. He argued that society was shaped by middle-class values (e.g. ambition and responsibility), and that these values were culturally transmitted through school and what it rewarded from students. Although lower-class boys tried to fit in with middle-class values, by getting jobs for example, they did not have the social ability to conform with those values fully. This led to social strain, as Merton had argued earlier. As a result, some of these boys formed gangs which deliberately rejected middle-class values. These subcultural gangs allowed status to be achieved through criminal acts, as an alternative means of obtaining the social respect which mainstream society would not allow them to achieve.

Similarly to Merton, Cohen classified three male groups according to whether the group members accepted middle-class values, and whether they had the ability to conform to those values. He called these:

- corner boys;
- college boys (who accepted and confirmed to middle class values); and
- delinquent boys (who formed the criminal gangs).

In Cohen's view, gangs with subcultural criminal values therefore provided a collective solution to the strain caused by unsuccessfully trying to comply with mainstream, middle-class social values. Cohen argued that the gangs which were formed as a result of this process were well-structured and well-organised, with clear leadership and identified roles for each member. His subcultural theory's innovation was to focus on gang behaviour and rejection of mainstream social values, as well as the importance of status and respect within these gangs.

Be critical

To be critical of Cohen's theory, you could again point to its reliance on official crime statistics, a problem shared by earlier sociological positivist theories such as strain theory. But you can – and should – try to analyse subcultural theory more deeply and specifically than this. For example, you could argue that the theory assumed that:

- lower-class boys always aspired to middle-class social values;
- middle-class values were always accepted throughout society; and
- cultural strain always led to crime – all of which makes the theory look slightly over-simplistic.

The theory did not consider the possibility that girls might form gangs and commit crime like boys. Its failure to consider female criminality made its ability to explain crime limited. Finally, other criminological research on subcultures (e.g. by cultural criminologists such as Mike Presdee) has indicated that they are not always as well-organised, as hierarchical, as gang-related or as criminally inclined as Cohen indicated.

✎ EXAM TIP

When critically discussing Cohen's work, you could question the overall contribution made by it to criminological theory overall, given that it shares so many of Merton's earlier concepts and values. Can it simply be written off as 'Merton with status'?

KEY THEORIST

Cloward and Ohlin's delinquency opportunity theory

Cloward and Ohlin, unlike Cohen, argued that only the less serious criminals were interested in obtaining social status through gangs. Like Merton, they claimed that more serious criminal gangs were mainly aimed at obtaining financial wealth. However, their **delinquency opportunity theory** argued that whether or not criminal subcultures were formed depended on how many opportunities there were for crime in a particular social environment – whether or not someone lived in an area where crime was common, for example, or knew others who committed crime.

Whereas Merton had argued that legitimate ways of obtaining financial success were unequally distributed in society, and therefore not available to everyone, Cloward and Ohlin claimed that opportunities for crime were also unequally distributed, and were not available to everyone. Cloward and Ohlin developed a typology of three different types of gang:

- criminal gangs who were focused on committing crime for financial reward;

- conflict gangs who were focused on obtaining social status and territory; and

- retreatist gangs who could not obtain social success legally, but did not want to obtain it illegally either.

Cloward and Ohlin's theory focused criminological attention on how criminal opportunities were unevenly distributed in society for the first time. It therefore tried to explain different forms of crime, including corporate crime as well as street crime such as drug-dealing and assault.

Be critical

Taking a critical approach, you could argue that the theory is too narrowly based, because it focuses its attention on lower-class criminals in what could be seen as a biased approach which overlooks crime committed by middle- and upper-class sections of society. You could also criticise the theory's assumption that everyone in society was motivated by financial gain, and that the young people in delinquent gangs always commit the same type of criminal behaviour – you could readily gather evidence from practical examples of gang-related crime in England and Wales to support this last point.

KEY THEORY

Labelling theory

Labelling theory centres on how people develop an image of themselves, and how that self-image is influenced by what others think of them. The nature of labels (e.g. 'criminal'), who applies them, how they are applied, and how labelling causes crime can then be studied. The emphasis of this theory is therefore on the response to crime, rather than criminal behaviour itself.

Edwin Lemert and Howard Becker argued that it was the criminal law which made behaviour criminal, and the response of criminal justice agencies such as the police and the courts which imposed the label of criminal on certain sections of society. It was the social response to an act of rule-breaking (primary deviation), and the labelling of this act as 'criminal' or 'wrong', which could lead to the rule-breaker reacting to being labelled by changing their self-image to fit in with this label (secondary deviation). The response of labelling then led to further criminal behaviour as the labelled person continued to live up to their label, and be further socially excluded as a result. Becker emphasised that a wide variety of individuals and groups in society had the ability to label others: not just criminal justice organisations, but also the media and other powerful people and groups.

Be critical

As with earlier sociological theories, you should consider the argument that labelling theory seems vague and over-simplistic in its explanations for crime – building on this, you could argue that it failed to make a full break with positivist values, and was not as radical an explanation for crime as it appeared to be. To support this view, you could argue that by not going further than stating that labelling occurs, and that deviance and crime results from labelling, the theory fails to explain the details of this process: why some people become labelled as deviant by society and others do not, and why some deviants become criminals and others do not.

The theory fails to explain what happens after the label has been applied, in terms of whether the person who has been labelled continues to behave in a deviant or criminal way, or whether being labelled deters them from further 'bad' behaviour. Also:

- the question of whether someone who has been labelled can ever get rid of the label is left unanswered by labelling theory; and

- labelling theory fails to address the issue of power relations in society, in terms of making it clear who has the power to label behaviour as 'criminal' or 'deviant', who has the power to maintain the presence of labels, and how this power operates.

✎ EXAM TIP

When analysing labelling theory critically, discussing the arguments of radical or Marxist criminology would add depth to the analysis, because it was radical criminology which attempted to fill the gap in labelling theory by focusing on how the powerful in society use their power to define (and commit) crime.

■ Sociological criminology's influences on criminal justice policy

The theories discussed in this chapter have had a considerable impact on criminal justice policy around the world, in the following particular ways:

- The work of the Chicago School encouraged governments and councils to spend money on improving social conditions in the most deprived geographical areas in Chicago itself, and the belief that crime can be reduced by doing this was still evident under the New Labour government in the UK in the late 1990s and early 2000s, as crime 'hot spots' such as council estates were the targets of investment in social facilities. The New Labour interest in communities as causes of, and the best way to respond to, crime can also be traced back to the Chicago School's geographical studies.

- As well as focusing criminological attention on corporate and white-collar crime for the first time, differential association theory arguably drives the policy of keeping young people and adults in separate prisons, to avoid older prisoners giving younger prisoners further ideas for committing crime.

- New Labour also used strain theory in their stated policy aim of improving opportunity for everyone in society – being 'tough on crime and tough on the causes of crime' in the words of Tony Blair – and although crime rates generally dropped during the New Labour administration, it was noticeable that the gap between rich and poor actually increased at this time in the UK.

- Finally, New Labour also made use of labelling theory in their attempts to clamp down on antisocial behaviour in the UK, especially in the use of antisocial behaviour orders (ASBOs) to criminalise types of behaviour which were not necessarily defined as crimes in the criminal law itself. The aim of ASBOs was to shame those who behaved badly and deter them from doing so – although Home Office research on ASBOs clearly showed that, for many young people, ASBOs were a badge of honour rather than a source of shame. This was a negative result for New Labour's policy, but a sign of support for the original labelling theory, since Becker had argued that if an individual or group was 'labelled' as criminal, they would accept the label through secondary deviation, and begin to live up to it by committing further crime.

■ Putting it all together

Answer guidelines

See the essay question at the start of the chapter.

Approaching the question

The question is asking you about how successful the various sociological theories of crime have been in breaking away from the assumption of positivism that internal biological or psychological factors predispose an individual to commit crime. You would therefore not only need to understand the principles of biological positivist criminology

▶

in order to answer the question fully, but would also need to critically analyse a range of sociological criminological theories in detail, to assess the extent to which they were successful in breaking away from positivistic determinism.

Important points to include

- Introduction mapping out the overall structure of the essay in brief.
- A detailed, critical analysis of positivist criminology's strengths but also a critique of the theory's weaknesses, for example an overly simplistic, deterministic view of why people commit crime.
- The Chicago School's environmental theory and its similarities and differences in relation to positivism.
- Sutherland's differential association theory and its similarities and differences in relation to positivism.
- Merton's strain theory and its similarities and differences in relation to positivism.
- Cohen's and Cloward and Ohlin's subcultural theories and their similarities and differences in relation to positivism.
- Lemert and Becker's labelling theory, and its similarities and differences in relation to positivism.
- Concluding paragraphs summarising the response to the question's assertion.

 Make your answer stand out

- Emphasise that social theories, if they are to explain crime fully, must always return to the idea of internal psychological processes (influenced by positivism) influencing the decision to commit crime, if they are not to fall into the trap of seeing people as robots with no control over their own actions.
- Use research evidence to argue in favour of or against the theories in the essay – for example, you could use British Crime Survey data to show that, contrary to positivist beliefs about the abnormality of crime and criminals, crime is a constant feature of social life.
- Show your knowledge of the evolution of strain theory in its various forms, such as the modern research of Agnew, and question the extent to which these modern variations meet the previous criticisms of Merton's work.

READ TO IMPRESS

Agnew, R. (1992) 'Foundation for a General Strain Theory', *Criminology,* **30**(1): 47–87.

Becker, H. (1963) *Outsiders: Studies in the sociology of deviance,* New York: Free Press.

Cloward, R.A. and Ohlin, L.E. (1960) *Delinquency and Opportunity: A theory of delinquent gangs.* New York: Free Press.

Merton, R.K. (1938) 'Social Structure and Anomie', *American Sociological Review,* **3**(5): 672–82.

Park, R.P., Burgess, E.W. and McKenzie, R.D. (1925) *The City: Suggestions for investigation of human behaviour in the urban environment,* Chicago, IL: University of Chicago Press.

Sutherland, E. (1949), *White – Collar Crime,* New York: Dryden Press.

www.pearsoned.co.uk/lawexpress

 Go online to access more revision support, including quizzes to test your knowledge, sample questions with answer guidelines, podcasts you can download, and more!

Contemporary criminology

9

Revision checklist

Essential points you should know:

- [ ] Marxist criminology and how it links crime to societal inequality
- [ ] Left realist criminology and how it differs from Marxist approaches
- [ ] Feminist criminologies, and their emphasis on gender divisions in society to explain crime
- [ ] Cultural criminology and its emphasis on 'crime as pleasure'
- [ ] Zemiological criminology and its focus on 'social harm'

■Topic map

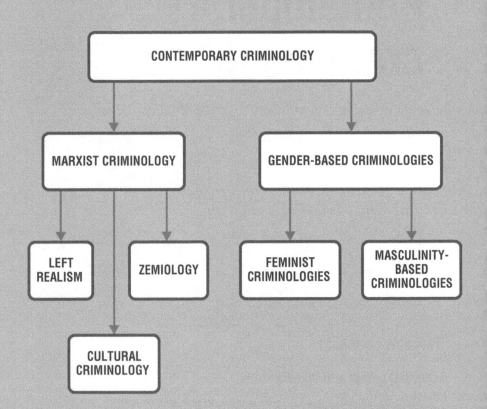

■ Introduction

In the past half century, a variety of new criminological theories have emerged.

While these new theories are often in direct opposition to one another in terms of their explanations for why crime occurs, they have all developed as a way of addressing what were perceived as flaws in the previous schools of criminological thought which have been discussed in previous chapters. In the exam setting, your main tasks when discussing contemporary criminology are to understand whether it offers anything new in terms of understanding crime, and how well it explains the reality of crime in contemporary society.

ASSESSMENT ADVICE

The theories in this chapter cover a range of theoretical ground, so essay and exam questions in this field will often ask you to compare and contrast the strengths and weaknesses of one theory against another where the two share some ideas in common – such as Marxism and left realism – rather than asking you to discuss the whole range of recent developments. Other assessment approaches centre on how easy these theories find it to explain the reality of crime in the present day.

■ Sample question

Could you answer this question? Below is a typical essay question that could arise on this topic. Guidelines on answering the question are included at the end of this chapter. Another sample question and guidance on tackling it can be found on the companion website.

ESSAY QUESTION

Critically discuss the idea that left realism can explain crime more effectively than Marxist criminology.

■ Key theorists and theories in contemporary criminology

📖 REVISION NOTE

Revise the theories in this chapter together with those in Chapter 8 to understand the roots of theory which considered society as a cause of crime in itself.

KEY DEFINITION: Contemporary criminology

A set of theoretical explanations for why crime occurs, which have emerged in the past 50 years or so, and which seek to build on and improve previous explanations of crime by refining them or by combining elements from one or more previous theories together.

KEY THEORY

Marxist criminology

Marxist writers such as Chambliss and Quinney argued that power, wealth and the means to produce the goods which society wants – as well as the means to define crime and define how criminal justice should operate – are concentrated in the hands of a small societal elite. Taylor, Walton and Young, in their book *The New Criminology*, claimed that the power to define and shape criminal law and criminal justice allowed the powerful to criminalise behaviour which threatened their power and interests, mask their own harmful activities (e.g. state or corporate crime) as non-criminal, and enabled them to protect and extend their social and financial power over the rest of society.

Marxist criminology criticised earlier criminological theory's failure to acknowledge that society is divided in terms of social class interests, that power and financial wealth are not equally distributed throughout society, and that only a few can exercise power through defining and enforcing the criminal law. Marxist criminology saw crime as being caused by a combination of the following:

- ever-expanding criminal law and criminal justice;
- political protest by the powerless against the powerful;
- divisions and inequality caused by capitalist society;
- individual selfishness and aggression encouraged by capitalism; and
- the deliberate deflection of society's fears of crime away from the crimes of the powerful and onto socially problematic and threatening lower-class behaviour.

All of these factors were seen by Marxists as being the result of the actions of the ruling-class elite.

✎ EXAM TIP

Emphasise in an exam how Marxist criminology focused on a range of criminological issues, from E.P. Thompson's critique of the historical widening of the criminal law by the ruling classes to protect their own interests, such as the redefinition of traditional working-class activities as crimes against property, to Stuart Hall's examination of how the media fuelled criminalisation by exaggerating the nature and seriousness of certain types of crime.

Make your answer stand out

Read Taylor et al. (1973) for the original full-scale application of Marxist theory to criminology, and Box (1983) for a more practical application of Marxist criminological theory to a range of different types of crime, including corporate crime, police crime and sexual offences.

Be critical

Use the arguments of left realists such as Jock Young (see below) to emphasise how Marxist criminologies tend towards deterministic over-simplification of the causes of crime, in an interesting mirror of the earlier positivist approach – whereas positivists explained crime purely in terms of individual difference, Marxism tended to explain it purely in terms of societal conditions. On the Marxist view, all crime was due to state power in the capitalist society – either in terms of the social and economic inequality which capitalism produced, the exploitation of the working class by the ruling class and the protest against this inequality which Marxists claimed resulted in crime, or the hiding of state and corporate crime which the power of the state allowed.

Left realists such as Jock Young made the following criticisms of the Marxist approach:

■ Marxism's over-simplistic view of the causes of crime ignored the messages from statistical and research data that not all crime was politically motivated, and that the majority of known crime was committed both by and against the working class.

■ Marxist criminology offered no practical suggestions for how the causes of crime could be tackled apart from ending capitalism (and even this idea ignored the fact that crime exists in non-capitalist countries as well).

■ Finally, Marxist criminology could be said to over-estimate the power and unity of interests of the ruling class in relation to law and crime.

KEY THEORY

Left realism

Left realist criminology grew out of the failure of Marxist or 'left idealist' criminology to acknowledge that most crime was not committed against the ruling class as a form of political protest. Drawing on empirical research in the form of victimisation surveys, as well as a range of earlier theories and ideas, left realism argued that, although social divisions along the lines of race, gender and class did help to cause crime, as the

▶

Marxists had argued (especially in the form of relative deprivation), the reality was that crime victimised the poorest in society the most, and that most offenders and victims were from a lower-class background. Therefore, criminology needed to explain this factor, take practical policy steps to help victims, and involve local communities in the response to crime, rather than trying to overthrow capitalism as the left idealists had suggested.

Left realist writers such as Jock Young (a former left idealist himself) argued that an effective theory of why crime occurred needed to take into account the whole of society and criminal justice, including the offender and the public as well as victims and the criminal justice system itself. As a result, while still taking societal inequality and discrimination into account as a cause of crime, left realism also took individual causes of crime into account, as well as the experiences of crime victims, in order to explain why both property and violent crime could and did increase even in times of economic prosperity, and in order to develop policies capable of reducing crime in practice.

 Make your answer stand out

To gain a deeper understanding of how left realism has developed, read and compare Jock Young's key article which rejected the earlier Marxist 'left idealism' in favour of a more realist approach (Young, 1986) with his later, more socially orientated work focusing on how social exclusion and its results trigger off crime (Young, 1999).

Be critical

To analyse left realism, an effective approach is to reverse the criticisms made by left realists against Marxism (see 'Be critical' box on p. 117). Use the arguments of Marxist criminologists to claim that left realism took the concept and definition of 'crime' for granted, as if crime was a fixed and readily identifiable concept on which there was a societal consensus, when in fact it constantly changed and evolved, and did so largely because of state power and how it was used.

Left realists were also criticised by Marxists for:

- assuming that offenders and victims were separate and distinct populations rather than overlapping populations;
- treating victim surveys as being a universally reliable indicator of victimisation;

- overlooking victims of crimes which were not linked with the working class (e.g. the victims of corporate or state crime); and

- advocating reform which was based around practical, narrow criminal justice measures rather than around changing wider social, political and economic structures which caused damaging social divisions and crime.

These criticisms can be summarised as an accusation that left realism 'sold out' too readily to liberal, mainstream ideas about the causes and nature of crime, and was therefore a regression from the radical, society-changing criminology of the Marxist radicals.

Left realism was also criticised by 'right realists'. **Right realism** shared left realism's focus on taking practical steps to tackle the causes of crime, but rejected the left realist view that tackling social inequality would do anything to address the causes of crime. Instead, leading right realists such as Charles Murray combined elements of biological positivism and individualist classicism to develop their theory of why crime occurred. They argued that, while crime was the result of individual calculation (and so the responses to crime should be based around deterrence and zero tolerance of any behaviour which was damaging to communities), a person's ability to calculate was driven by their biological and genetic traits. This biosocial theory critiqued left realism's acceptance of social and structural causes of crime, such as poverty and racism.

✎ EXAM TIP

Left realism's emphasis on pragmatic measures to tackle the causes of crime offers considerable scope for discussion and critical analysis of research which was influenced by left realist theory – you should therefore use literature of this kind, such as local victim surveys, to assess the effectiveness of its approach.

KEY THEORY

Feminist criminologies

A range of criminologies focusing on the importance of gender in explaining and understanding crime have emerged since the 1970s. **Feminist criminologies** criticised mainstream criminology for ignoring the fact that men seem to commit more crime than women on the basis of crime and sentencing statistics, for stereotyping women who commit crime as either 'mad' or 'evil', for ignoring the discrimination faced by women in society which caused crime, and for ignoring the experiences of women in relation to crime generally.

Writers such as Carol Smart (1976) argued that women who committed crime were seen as being doubly deviant: they were not only punished for committing crime, but also for breaking the sexist stereotyping of women's appropriate behaviour as being passive and gentle. Later feminist criminologists, such as Frances Heidensohn (1996), claimed that women commit less crime because they are under greater social control than men (through the family and education), and that understandings of female crime were affected by stereotyped assumptions about typical female behaviour (so that shoplifting is often wrongly seen as being primarily a female crime). Feminist criminologies therefore sought to understand the perspectives of women involved in crime, and to locate the meanings of gender in relation to crime within the context of wider gender-based discrimination in different aspects of society, especially in terms of labour, power and sexuality divisions.

❗ Don't be tempted to . . .

Avoid referring to one universal 'feminist criminology' in essay or exam answers. There have always been a series of feminist perspectives in relation to criminology, ranging from liberal feminism (citing differing gender socialisation as the cause of crime, and aiming for gender equality) through radical and Marxist feminism (which focuses on male patriarchy and capitalism-generated social gender inequality as the causes of crime) to postmodernist perspectives which abandoned what they saw as over-generalised large-scale theory in favour of explaining crime through the individual perspectives of offenders, and deconstructing the idea of 'crime' itself into social problems. All of these schools of thought place the focus on the relationship between women and crime, and on questions of gender representations in society, but there are noticeable differences between them in terms of how they explain crime.

Make your answer stand out

Smart's (1976) book was a very influential critique of mainstream criminology according to feminist principles, while Heidensohn (1996) is a theoretically informed discussion of why women seem to commit far less crime than men.

Be critical

You need to take a varied and multi-faceted approach to critically analysing feminist theory, remembering that there are a range of feminist theories, rather than just one. Feminist criminologies cover so much theoretical ground that you need to remember which type you are aiming criticism at. To give one example of how you could include this specific analysis, left realism was critical of postmodernist feminist criminology for its inconsistent and destructive approach to criminology: criticising mainstream criminology for treating crime as a fixed concept while treating key feminist issues such as rape as a fixed, beyond-criticism concept themselves, and taking an overly-cynical approach to criminological theory.

✎ EXAM TIP

To assess the impact of feminist criminologies, you could bring masculinity-based criminologies into an exam question. **Masculinity criminologies** have criticised feminist criminologies for focusing too much on women in a one-dimensional way, rather than focusing on why men commit so much crime, particularly violent crime. Writers such as Connell and Messerschmidt focus on how social structures and economic inequalities produce different types of masculinity, encourage men to be aggressive and violent, and therefore explain why most (male-committed) crime occurs.

KEY THEORY

Cultural criminology

The cultural criminologists viewed crime, its meaning and its causes as cultural constructs. They were particularly interested in the idea of crime as an expressive or emotional activity, and as an attempt to escape from the repression of particular types of culture by the powerful in society. **Cultural criminology** argued that a 'hyper-capitalist' society which emphasised the importance of work led to people seeking pleasure in semi-legal or illegal activities, and developing their own cultural meanings as a result. Crime could provide emotional excitement through the 'buzz' of committing illegal and pleasurable activities, often in the context of wider cultures.

In conflict with this pleasure-seeking behaviour, though, was a dominant mainstream society, governed by the interests of the powerful within it, which tried to criminalise certain 'problematic' cultural activities through the use of criminal law and criminal justice to repress those activities and condemn those who pursued pleasure as 'outsiders'. As a result, for example, consenting to violence in a sport such as boxing is defined as legal and even desirable by mainstream society, but consenting to sadomasochism for sexual pleasure is criminalised. These attempts at criminalising cultures, however, made those cultures more exciting and attractive to those whose behaviour was being repressed, a process which was exacerbated by the media's frequent use of illegal or semi-legal behaviour as a marketing tool to sell various products to capitalist consumers. Cultural criminology, therefore, draws on a range of older criminologies in an attempt to explain social and cultural attitudes towards crime in modern-day, media-saturated society.

Be critical

You should critique how socially aware cultural criminology really is. You could do this, for example, by arguing that cultural criminology overemphasises some social factors in explaining crime – namely the cultural dimension of why crime occurs – but fails to give enough attention to social factors in crime such as social divisions and economic inequality (you could additionally identify these social factors as phenomena which often determine how cultural meanings are interpreted by individuals).

Cultural criminology has been criticised for assuming that all subcultures are exciting, risky and publicly displayed (e.g. some cultural transgressive behaviour happens in private).

It has also been argued that cultural criminology risks romanticising harmful and morally questionable criminal behaviour, just because it is committed in the context of an alternative, repressed subculture.

✎ EXAM TIP

To analyse cultural criminology more deeply in an exam, try to unravel its criminological influences in older theories – labelling and subcultural theories, for example – and use these to question whether cultural criminology really offers anything new in theoretical terms.

KEY THEORY

Zemiology

Zemiology explicitly goes beyond criminology in its search for the causes of criminal behaviour – in fact, it argues that criminology does not and cannot explain why crime occurs, for a number of reasons:

- focusing on 'crime' itself just hides the fact that 'crime' cannot be objectively defined;

- mainstream criminology legitimises the distorted picture of crime as being more serious than most of it actually is while ignoring serious harms such as state crime; and

- mainstream criminology wrongfully accepts the ineffectiveness of criminal justice, therefore allowing the making of profit through crime (e.g. private prisons) to expand and reproducing the maintenance of power inequality and social control.

Zemiologists widen their focus to all activities which can be seen as socially harmful – not only officially defined 'criminal behaviour' itself, but also poor healthcare, poor education and social inequality – so as to find the causes of these problems. Zemiologists therefore see 'crime' as it is legally defined as just one of a range of social problems, all of which should be addressed and punished in a just and equal society. Such a holistic approach has led zemiologists to study such issues as poverty and homophobia as causes of social harm.

Zemiologists view the causes of crime and other social problems as being due to social inequality along the lines of gender, race, class and sexuality, as well as due to the maintenance of the socio-economic interests of the ruling-class elite. As such, zemiology uses similar causal explanations for crime to Marxist criminology, while effectively advocating the dismantling of criminology as a distinct social discipline, in line with a postmodernist approach.

Make your answer stand out

Hillyard et al. (2004) explain the basic principles of the 'social harm' approach, and applies it to a range of social policy issues as well as to particular aspects of crime itself, in a deliberate and direct challenge to criminology as a distinct academic discipline.

✎ EXAM TIP

Be careful, when discussing zemiology, to focus on its particular application to the causes and incidence of crime, rather than discussing social policy in a broader and more generic sense, which is likely to make your answer lose focus and relevance.

Be critical

You could argue that the zemiological approach fails to advance criminological theory any further than previous theories, because it replaces one set of problems – defining what 'crime' is and explaining it on that basis, as mainstream criminology attempts to do – with another, namely how to define and measure what counts as 'social harm', which could be seen as just as much a subjective concept as 'crime' itself. You could also consider the extent to which zemiology tends to fall back on structural socio-economic factors as explanations for why crime and other social harms occur – if you accept this line of argument, it then opens the door for you to use the same criticisms as Marxist criminology has faced in your essay or exam.

■ Contemporary criminology's influences on criminal justice policy

The criminological theories discussed in this chapter have not had the same level of influence on criminal justice policy as the older theories discussed in previous chapters. In some cases, this is because they are too new to have had the opportunity to influence policy (e.g. cultural criminology and zemiology):

■ Marxist criminology deliberately distanced itself from what it saw as mainstream criminology which only reinforced and protected the interests of the ruling class. It also saw attempts at reforming criminal justice as pointless unless capitalism itself was removed from society. This has meant that any impact Marxist theory has had on policy has been in relation to pressure groups campaigning against the misuse of state power, such as INQUEST, a group which challenges government policy on inquests into deaths in police and prison custody. You should note that Marxist-influenced criminology has been more influential in other countries than in England and Wales – Thomas Mathiesen's abolitionist strategy had the effect of greatly reducing the prison population in Norway, for example.

■ The realist theories have had a significantly greater influence on policy than the other theories in this chapter, because their pragmatism and emphasis on realistic reform made them very suitable for use in short – and medium – term criminal justice policy. The New Labour government which took office in 1997 initially showed a commitment to left realist-style approaches which recognised the link between social inequality and crime, such as the Sure Start scheme aimed at diverting young children away from criminal behaviour, and also tried to give communities a greater role in the response to crime, as left realism had advocated, through the introduction of criminal justice multi-agency partnerships in the Crime and Disorder Act 1998.

■ However, there was also a right realist influence on New Labour's criminal justice policies which emphasised a more punitive approach to crime and saw crime as the result of free will – the introduction of ASBOs to combat 'antisocial behaviour' which did not necessarily amount to officially defined crime in the Crime and Disorder Act 1998, the lengthening of criminal sentences based on deterrence (e.g. the incapacitative sentencing for violent or sexual offences in the Criminal Justice Act 2003), and various policies emphasising individual responsibility for crime all carry the influence of right realism.

■ Putting it all together

Answer guidelines

See the essay question at the start of the chapter.

Approaching the question

This question is asking you to compare and contrast the abilities of two theories to explain crime – Marxist criminology and left realism. In answering the question, you need to remember that left realism developed from Marxist roots, and acknowledge that supporters of each theory have criticised each other in an ongoing theoretical and policy debate.

Important points to include

■ Introduction briefly introducing the basic concepts of Marxist and left realist criminology.

■ Discussion of Marxist criminology's explanations for why crime occurs: exploitation, mystification and over-criminalisation.

■ Critical analysis of Marxist criminology's weaknesses in terms of explaining crime, for example denial of individual responsibility.

- Discussion of left realism's explanations for why crime occurs, for example relative deprivation.
- Critical analysis of left realism's weaknesses in explaining crime, for example the treatment of 'crime' as a fixed concept.
- Conclusion reaching decision on which theory can explain crime more effectively.

 Make your answer stand out

- Emphasise the range of applications used by Marxist criminology, covering crimes committed by the powerful, causes of crime in history and processes of criminalisation, to demonstrate its flexibility as a theory.
- Evaluate the theoretical journey taken by left realism in terms of explaining crime (e.g. Jock Young's moves towards structural and cultural approaches in his recent academic work).
- Emphasise each theory's links to policy, not just in terms of its level of engagement with policy, but also in terms of its ability to maintain academic integrity when transferred into policy (e.g. left realism's propensity to blur with right realism in New Labour's criminal justice policy).

READ TO IMPRESS

Box, S. (1983) *Power, Crime and Mystification,* London: Routledge.

Heidensohn, F. (1996) *Women and Crime* (2nd edn.), Basingstoke: Macmillan.

Hillyard, P., Pantazis, C., Tombs, S. and Gordon, D. (eds.) (2004) *Beyond Criminology: Taking harm seriously,* London: Pluto Press.

Presdee, M. (2000) *Cultural Criminology and the Carnival of Crime,* London: Routledge.

Smart, C. (1976) *Women, Crime and Criminology: A feminist critique,* London: Routledge and Kegan Paul.

Taylor, I., Walton, P. and Young, J. (1973) *The New Criminology: For a social theory of deviance,* London: Routledge and Kegan Paul.

Young, J. (1986) 'The Failure of Criminology: The need for a radical realism', in Young, J. and Matthews, R. (eds.) *Confronting Crime,* London: Sage.

Young, J. (1999) *The Exclusive Society,* London: Sage.

www.pearsoned.co.uk/lawexpress

 Go online to access more revision support, including quizzes to test your knowledge, sample questions with answer guidelines, podcasts you can download, and more!

10

Theories of justice and penology

Revision checklist

Essential points you should know:

- [ ] The key theoretical approaches to justifying why punishment occurs – reductivism, retributivism and reparation
- [ ] The key theoretical approaches to explaining how punishment operates – the ideas of writers such as Durkheim, Weber, Elias, Foucault and Garland, as well as the Marxist penologists
- [ ] How theories of justice and punishment have influenced criminal justice policy

■Topic map

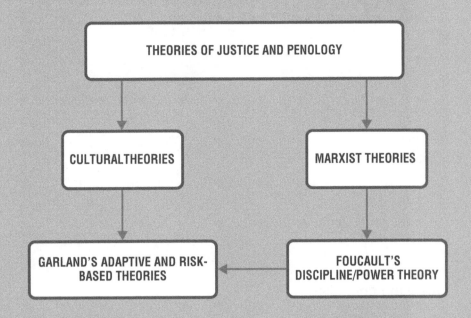

■ Introduction

There are two key analytical issues relating to the study of criminal punishment – or penology – which you will need to show awareness of in an exam question.

Firstly, there are several justifications for criminal punishment, each of which has had an influence on punishment policy. These have come from law-based studies into punishment. Secondly, there are several explanations for why and how punishment has operated, and does operate, each of which focus on the societal context in which punishment is used as a way of explaining the practice of punishment. These explanatory ideas have come from a sociological approach to studying punishment. A fully analytical exam answer on punishment should take into account both the legal and the sociological dimensions of penology.

ASSESSMENT ADVICE

Essay and exam questions on punishment might ask you to relate a particular justification for punishment to criminal justice policy and practice relating to punishment, in terms of assessing how influential a particular justification for punishment has been on policy and practice. Questions might also ask you about how effective the different sociological explanations for punishments are in terms of explaining how punishment currently works in practice.

■ Sample question

Could you answer this question? Below is a typical essay question that could arise on this topic. Guidelines on answering the question are included at the end of this chapter. Another sample question and guidance on tackling it can be found on the companion website.

ESSAY QUESTION

Are any of the theories which attempt to explain punishment capable of explaining current developments in penological policy and practice in England and Wales?

■ Key theorists and theories in the justification of punishment

> **KEY DEFINITION:** Justificatory theories of punishment
>
> A set of theoretical rationales and justifications for the nature of punishment in, based on the perceived fairness and/or efficiency of a punishment system which conforms to the beliefs included as part of these theories.

> **KEY THEORY**
>
> *Reductivism*
>
> **Reductivism** is based around the idea that punishment can be justified by its ability to prevent crime from happening again in the future. There are several different forms of reductivist justification for punishment.

Firstly, **deterrence** involves putting people off committing crime through either a sentence of punishment which they themselves have received and found to be unpleasant (individual deterrence), or through seeing the unpleasant effects of punishment on other people (general deterrence). Deterrence theorists argue that the pain of punishment is justified as long as the punishment avoids further pain to others in the future, but writers such as Jeremy Bentham argued that only the minimum amount of punishment necessary to produce deterrence should be used. Bentham argued that punishment should aim to achieve the greatest happiness for the greater number of people, and that its nature and extent should be measured by the 'felicific calculus', taking into account issues such as how severe the pain of punishment was compared to the pleasure of committing crime, and how quickly the pain will be generated.

Secondly, **rehabilitation** is the idea that an offender can be 'cured' of wanting to reoffend, and reintegrated into society, by forced treatment, given as part of the punishment imposed through sentencing. Sentences that were longer than what would be proportionate to criminal responsibility for the offence would be justifiable under a rehabilitation-based approach, depending on how long it took each individual offender to be rehabilitated.

The final form of reductivist punishment is **incapacitation**. This approach focuses on identifying those who pose the greatest risk of reoffending in the future, and protecting the public from their reoffending by physically preventing them from committing crime – by sending them to prison or disqualifying them from driving, for example.

📖 **REVISION NOTE**

When discussing the principles of deterrence, link back to the ideas of classicist criminology which were discussed in Chapter 5. Deterrence's values are closely linked with the ideas of classicists such as Beccaria and Bentham. On the other hand, the ideas behind rehabilitation are closely linked with positivist criminology, which was discussed in Chapters 6 and 7.

 Make your answer stand out

Walker (1991) is a defence of deterrence, which blends theoretical and evidence-based arguments and acts as a powerful critique of just deserts-based punishment systems (see below) – critically analyse its arguments against basing punishment about rights.

Be critical

As is often the case in critical analysis, an effective way of critiquing reductivist theory is to consider the extent to which research evidence shows that it works in practice – in other words, that it does what it claims to do to offenders. You could argue, in support of this, that all three main reductivist justifications for punishment have struggled to prove, in the light of reoffending statistics for different types of punishment, that they are guaranteed to prevent future offending in every single case of punishment (e.g. von Hirsch's research indicated that there was no definitive evidence that harsher punishments produced greater deterrence).

Reductivist approaches also face several other problematic ethical issues:

■ they would potentially allow the punishment of innocent people, if the goals of deterrence or incapacitation dictated it;

■ they would potentially punish people in a disproportionate, potentially unlimited way if that was required to, for example, enable rehabilitation; and

■ in the case of incapacitation, they would allow people to be punished on the grounds of crime which they have not committed yet.

Retributivism

Retributivism justifies punishment through sentencing on the ground that it is deserved by the offender. Unlike reductivism, it 'looks back' to the offence which has been committed to justify punishment. On this view, punishment is justified because people have made the voluntary choice to commit crime. Therefore, convicted criminals are morally responsible for their actions, and should be blamed, and censured by the state in the form of punishment, as a result.

Retributivism can therefore be seen as a way of communicating the fact that the offender has done something wrong, and in turn, the offender accepts society's ideas about what is right and wrong by undergoing the punishment. However, retributivists also say that offenders should only be blamed and punished to a level proportionate with the extent to which it is fair to blame them for what they have done, and with the seriousness of the offence of which they have been convicted and no further (unlike reductivism). This approach is known as 'just deserts' sentencing, and is linked with the idea of proportionality between an offence and the way in which it is punished. This includes ordinal proportionality (comparably serious offences should receive comparably serious sentences) and cardinal proportionality (the setting of the overall level of punishment).

 Make your answer stand out

Academic discussion of retributivism has been closely linked with liberal theories of how punishment should operate which focus on individual responsibility for crime and the principles of balancing maximum individual freedom from legal intervention with universal equality for everyone. Read the work of von Hirsch (1976) for a deeper understanding of the philosophy of retributivist punishment.

Be critical

You should use retributivism's own claims to be a just and consistent method of punishment to critically analyse its effectiveness as a way of punishing offenders. For example, you could point out that retributivism's claim that sentences must be proportional to crimes does not tell us about how the sentencing tariff will be set out – in other words, how offences should be arranged in order of seriousness, or what the start and end points of the sentencing scale should be. As with reductivism above, you need to relate the theory to evidence of how (and how well) retributivism is likely to work in terms of punishment in practice.

Other criticisms of retributivism include:

- The basic principles of retributivism do not tell us how, and how exactly, sentences should be measured against crimes.

- Punishing on the basis that the community and/or the state have a moral right to censure and punish offenders for what they have done could be seen as no more than state-sponsored revenge against offenders – if it is seen in this way, retributive sentencing does not have the moral content that it claims to have.

- Critical penologists have claimed that, in an unequal capitalist society, the state lacks the moral right to punish people, and that retributive punishment ignores inequality and social deprivation by claiming to punish people equally.

✎ EXAM TIP

Give added depth to your critique of liberal and retributive justifications for punishment by referring to the arguments put forward by communitarian writers who believe that communities have shared moral values, the breach of which should justify punishment, and that communities are the best forum for carrying out punishment – Duff's ideas on punishment as a form of moral communication between communities and offenders, with formal criminal justice ensuring that fairness and the rights of offenders are respected by community justice, are an example of the communitarian approach.

! Don't be tempted to . . .

Avoid arguing that reductivism and retributivism are entirely irreconcilable justifications for punishments. For example, von Hirsch's later work argues that, once the value of punishment has been chosen retributively, the sentence which was most likely to promote crime prevention should be chosen in line with reductivist values; Carlen has argued in favour of retributive proportionate sentences which have reductivist rehabilitative content; and Cavadino and Dignan see fundamental human rights as dictating retributivist limits on punishment, while leading to punishment in line with reductivist crime prevention to promote freedom of choice for all in society.

KEY THEORY

Reparation

Reparation, or restorative justice, is different from both retribution and reductivism as a sentencing strategy. Reparation focuses on the offender making amends in some way to the victim of the offence, through various forms of punishment, for the harm which the victim has suffered.

Reparation aims to bring the offender and victim together to work out how to resolve the conflict caused by the crime. It therefore 'looks back' to the harm caused by crime, as retributivism does, but also 'looks forward' to how that harm can be repaired, and how the offender can be reintegrated back into society after being 'shamed' for committing the offence, in the style of reductivism.

 Make your answer stand out

Read and use the ideas of Braithwaite (1989) for a better understanding of the principles of restorative justice, especially the key concept of reintegrative shaming, whereby the offender is 'shamed' by punishment but then reintroduced back into the community without further stigma.

✎ EXAM TIP

Use practical evidence of how effective restorative justice has been in practice to show not only the possible limitations of its effectiveness as a theory, but also the wide range of practical techniques of applying it that exist.

Be critical

The main criticism which you could target at reparation as a method of punishment in an essay or exam answer is the fact that it lacks coherence in terms of how it should operate in policy and practice – simply comparing and contrasting different writers' definitions of reparation or restorative justice would give evidence to support this point. Beyond its basic aims of repairing the harm caused by crime, and of giving victims a more central role in the process of punishment, there is a lack of consensus as to how restorative justice can justify and reform the process of punishment.

Reparation is also criticised because:

- empirical evidence that restorative justice can be effective in terms of reducing crime is mixed – possibly because of the lack of consensus on the best ways to use it;

- reparation often carries with it an assumption that offenders and victims are different and discrete groups of people within society, when research evidence suggests that it is perfectly possible, and in fact normal, for people to be offenders and victims;

- there is a danger that reparation can over-prioritise the rights of either offenders or victims, excluding the other side; and

- it is debatable whether it is possible (or desirable) for restorative justice to be used as part of a coercive punishment system without compromising on its essential principles.

▪ Key theorists and theories in the explanation of punishment

KEY DEFINITION: Explanatory theories of punishment

A set of theoretical explanations for the nature of punishment in a particular time or place, and its past and future development, based on past and current evidence on the development of punishment in a particular time and place.

KEY THEORIST

Émile Durkheim

Durkheim saw punishment as being vital to the creation and maintenance of solidarity in society. He viewed punishment as being a vital means of maintaining order, solidarity and obedience to law in society, and recognised punishment's emotional and expressive functions. His work was therefore an example of **cultural penology**.

In Durkheim's view, the nature of crime and punishment changed as societies changed from pre-industrial to industrialised. In pre-industrial societies, crime was seen as being against God and therefore shocking to society generally, and punishments tended to reflect society's outraged response to crime by being severe and corporal in nature in order to reinforce the collective consciousness. However, as societies became more industrialised, state and religious power declined. As a result, there was more sympathy for offenders and, although punishment was still needed to reinforce the collective consciousness and maintain social order, changes in society meant that it was not as harsh as before.

KEY THEORIST

Max Weber

Weber viewed religion and culture as being just as important as the economy in terms of their influence on society and punishment. His typologies of the different types of authority which can be obtained by the powerful in society have been particularly relevant to penology. Weber argued that there were three models of authority:

- traditional – hereditary rulers governing as of right and according to tradition;

- charismatic – rulers governing through their own charisma and personality; and

- rational – legal – authority through systematic rules and bureaucratic organisation.

Weber claimed that the rational – legal type of authority was the most valuable and stable, and that its emergence in modern societies was the result of stronger and more centralised forms of government. The importance to Weber of government managerialism, bureaucracy and rationality in punishment, and the centralisation of power, was influential over later thinkers such as Foucault (see below).

KEY THEORIST

Norbert Elias

Elias applied the concept of increasing civilisation to society generally and to punishment in particular. Elias argued that, from the Middle Ages onwards, societies became more self-restrained and self-controlled in their behaviour, in a number of different ways. As governments became more powerful and centralised, so there was less violence in society, and less need for self-expression. For the purposes of punishment, Elias believed that punishments became less public, less physical and more efficient (rather than more 'civilised' in the usual sense of the word) as the civilisation process continued.

Be critical

You could improve the conciseness of your analysis in this area by pointing to the values (and theoretical weaknesses) which all three writers above have in common, in line with the analytical approach taken by Garland (1990). All of the three explanations are based around the links between societal culture and forms of punishment and, although Garland supports the cultural aspect of punishment, and Elias's civilising process, he criticises Durkheim and Weber for ignoring punishment's role in reflecting and maintaining power relationships and social control, and serving the needs of the powerful, within societies.

Durkheim's work has also been accused of confusing the functions of punishment with explanations for why and how it has developed, and of inaccuracy in terms of its claims that punishment would continually become less and less punitive as societies became more modernised – harsh punishments, such as extensive prison use, still feature significantly in modern-day societies. John Pratt has argued that punishment is now becoming 'decivilised' again, contrary to Elias's argument, in the form of offenders doing community service being made to wear fluorescent jackets to make them more noticeable to the public for example.

KEY THEORY

Marxist theories

Marxist penology is focused on the economic structures and processes of production within a particular society at a given time, the social inequality inherent in capitalist societies, and the oppression of working-class people by middle- and upper-class people. Marxist penologists explain punishment by seeing it as a method of maintaining the current social order and the interests of the powerful, in line with social and economic conditions. This means that the economic structure of society, as governed by the powerful in that society, determines the shape of punishment.

There are a range of important Marxist penologists. For example:

- Rusche and Kirchheimer argued that each society's ruling class found ways of punishing which suited its economic interests, so that penal practice is directly and deterministically driven by a society's economic needs at any given time – so, since capitalism relies on the labour of the working class, prison was more effective than corporal or capital forms of punishment.

- Gramsci argued that punishment was a means by which the powerful in society attempted to achieve a hegemonic dominance of their own ideological values through a mixture of coercion and persuasion, although this hegemony could be overcome through the efforts of individuals.

- Althusser claimed that punishment, like the rest of society, was structurally caused by the economic needs of the powerful, and that it acted as a means both of repressing rebellion against the ruling class and of reproducing ruling-class ideologies for their own benefit.

- E.P. Thompson argued that the powerful in society used their power to define and shape the criminal law, and so used punishment as a means of attempting to control the working class by criminalising activities which were seen as a threat to their power – but he also thought that the powerless had the ability to control their own lives to some extent, and to fight back against, and in some cases resist, these attempts to control their behaviour.

📖 REVISION NOTE

Use the discussion of Marxist criminology in Chapter 9 to help you understand the different Marxist approaches to explaining punishment.

Be critical

The most obvious approach to critically analysing Marxist approaches is on the grounds of their most fundamental belief – namely, the deterministic assumption of a causal relationship between economic conditions and forms of punishment, and the corresponding denial that individuals outside the ruling class have any control or choice about how punishment is carried out. You could criticise this belief from a number of different academic viewpoints, as positivist (biological and psychological), feminist and sociological theories of crime have all critically analysed Marxist penology on this ground. You would therefore have a wide range of evidence to choose from in support of your argument.

Some Marxist approaches, such as those of Gramsci and E.P. Thompson, meet the above criticism by moving away from determinism and focusing on the role of ideology and obtaining societal support for punishment by consensus. However, you could then argue in your essay or exam answer that these approaches move so far away from orthodox Marxist penology that they are not essentially Marxist at all, beyond a basic consideration of the links between material conditions and punishment in society.

KEY THEORIST

Michel Foucault

Foucault was influenced by Marxism, but did not agree with the orthodox Marxist view that economic conditions influenced forms of punishment in a deterministic way. By analysing the history of punishment, Foucault argued that punishment changed from being corporal (corporal and capital punishment) to carceral (the prison) because it was more economically profitable for the powerful to discipline and monitor offenders, and to retrain them as 'good' citizens, than to kill or injure them through punishment.

Prison was then used to discipline offenders psychologically rather than physically, through constant surveillance, training and strict daily routines. Foucault argued that prison failed in its bid to reform offenders, but that it continued to be used because it was useful to the powerful in retaining their power over the rest of society. Foucault also argued that punishment (not in prisons, but through other social institutions such as schools too) allowed the powerful to increase their power through gathering knowledge about offenders, seeing power and knowledge as being closely linked, although he saw power as being the subject of contests and struggles throughout society.

✎ EXAM TIP

Foucault's ideas can be difficult to understand and explain, so use some alternative sources to explain his ideas more clearly. Cohen's (1985) use of the concepts of net-widening, mesh-thinning, blurring and penetration to describe how community penalties were a vehicle for greater **social control** and discipline, and how they were extending the punitiveness of prison further and deeper into the fabric of society, were heavily influenced by Foucault, and so represents a key source for explaining Foucault's ideas.

Be critical

Foucault bases his ideas on historical evidence, so the reliability of his theories depends on the accuracy with which he interprets the historical development of punishment. You would be well-advised in essay or exam answers on Foucault to argue that the accuracy of his historical analysis, suggesting a clear-cut penological transformation from death penalty to prison, is over-simplistic and ignores the variable effects of punishment on individuals, as well as variations in penal policy in different locations.

You could also use the work of more modern writers such as David Garland to criticise Foucault's over-emphasis on the physical aspect of punishment and his converse under-emphasis of the emotional and expressive functions of punishment. Garland also argued that Foucault and his followers have over-estimated the ability of punishment, surveillance and social control to affect people's lives in a negative way.

■ Theories of justice and penology's influences on criminal justice policy

Thinking firstly about theories which attempt to justify punishment, both retributivist and reductivist theories have played important roles in sentencing policy at different times:

■ The Criminal Justice Act 1991, with its emphasis on proportionality between crime and sentence and removal of past convictions from sentencing consideration, was strongly influenced by retributivism – although some of its retributivist elements were removed by later legislation, and even the original 1991 Act contained provision for reductivist disproportionate, deterrent and incapacitative sentences for violent and sexual offenders.

■ In more recent times, reductivism has become far more prominent in sentencing policy, with the introduction of deterrent punishments such as antisocial behaviour orders in the Crime and Disorder Act 1998, and indeterminate incapacitative sentences for 'dangerous' offenders in the Criminal Justice Act 2003.

■ That said, the 2003 Act still contains a requirement of proportionality in sentencing – showing that retributivism and reductivism both play a competing role in current policy.

Turning to explanations for punishment, David Garland has argued that all of the explanations discussed in this chapter play a part in explaining punishment, but that no one theory can explain the entirety of punishment by itself. Drawing on the cultural explanations of Durkheim, Weber and Elias, but also on the social control and discipline theories of Foucault, Garland argues that culture (including factors like ideas about what justice means and about society itself) influence the nature of punishment, but that the state's sense of penal crisis based on the criminal justice landscape in late modernity (e.g. continually high crime rates, a move towards actuarial assessment of criminal risk, and acceptance that crime cannot be wiped out completely) influences punishment as well.

The result, in Garland's view, has been a 'culture of control', with apparently contradictory penal policies: expressive on the one hand (denials of the limits to what punishment can do about crime and calls for more punitiveness and incapacitation, plus symbolic, knee-jerk policies such as mandatory sentences), adaptive on the other (e.g. devolving responsibility for punishment away from the state and onto private agencies). Garland's approach is a theory based on practical evidence of how he sees punishment as working currently, and can explain such contemporary features of punishment as ever-increasing imprisonment rates in England and Wales, which have risen from 40,000 in 1992 to over 85,000 in 2011 (expressive strategy) and the privatisation of punishment agencies such as prisons (adaptive strategy).

■ Putting it all together

Answer guidelines

See the essay question at the start of the chapter.

Approaching the question

This question is asking you to compare and contrast the strengths and weaknesses of the different explanations of punishment, but it is also asking you to link them with current developments in penal policy in England and Wales. You therefore need to critique each theory with reference to these policy developments, as well as with reference to other competing theories.

Important points to include

- Introduction briefly showing awareness of the competing explanations for why punishment has worked, and does work, in practice, and briefly mapping out the different types of punishment which exist.

- Discussion and critique of cultural penal theories, including those of Durkheim, Weber and Elias, and relation of these theories to current penal developments.

- Discussion and critique of Marxist penal theories, and relation of these theories to current penal developments.

- Discussion and critique of Foucault's penal theory, and relation of this theory to current penal developments.

- Discussion and critique of Garland's pluralist and 'culture of control' theories, and relation of these theories to current penal developments.

- Conclusion reaching decision on whether any of the theories can explain current trends on its own.

Make your answer stand out

- Discuss and critique a range of Marxist theories rather than just giving one example – the differences between them are important in terms of their relative explanatory power.

- Although the question is about explanations for punishment rather than justifications for it, make links between the two aspects of penology in your answer, for example between the 'risk management' model and reductivist approaches of incapacitation and deterrence.

- Be critical with Garland's theories – don't be tempted to accept his ideas uncritically simply because his 'culture of control' theory claims to be based around current evidence on punishment.

READ TO IMPRESS

Braithwaite, J. (1989) *Crime, Shame and Reintegration,* Cambridge: Cambridge University Press.

Cohen, S. (1985) *Visions of Social Control,* Cambridge: Polity Press.

Duff, R.A. (2003) *Punishment, Communication and Community,* Oxford: Oxford University Press.

Garland, D. (1990) *Punishment and Modern Society,* Oxford: Clarendon.

Garland, D. (2001) *The Culture of Control,* Oxford: Oxford University Press.

von Hirsch, A. (1976) *Doing Justice: The choice of punishments,* New York: Hill and Wang.

Walker, N. (1991) *Why Punish?,* Oxford: Oxford University Press.

www.pearsoned.co.uk/lawexpress

 Go online to access more revision support, including quizzes to test your knowledge, sample questions with answer guidelines, podcasts you can download, and more!

And finally, before the exam . . .

Having read through the earlier chapters in this book, you should now be in a position, not only to show detailed understanding and knowledge of the key topic areas within criminology, but also to show understanding of the complex ways in which these topics relate to each other.

Finally, you should be able to apply your knowledge of key criminological theorists, theories and sources in an exam setting, whether you are asked to complete an essay or a problem-style question:

- Remember that criminology is a subject where there can be more than one right answer to a question. There are many different valid perspectives on issues such as what causes crime. It is up to you, in an exam, to construct an argument which supports a particular position. Don't forget to back your argument up with evidence though, and to reflect its weaknesses as well as its strengths.

- When discussing a theory of crime, always think about where that theory came from (i.e. which other theories influenced it), and how that theory has in turn influenced other, later theories. This will help you to remember and show knowledge of the links between different theories in the exam setting.

- Always look for and use evidence of how different criminological theories have translated into criminal justice policy in England and Wales.

Test yourself

☐ Look at the **revision checklists** at the start of each chapter. Are you happy that you can now tick them all? If not, go back to the particular chapter and work through the material again. If you are still struggling, seek help from your tutor.

☐ Attempt the **sample questions** in each chapter and check your answers against the guidelines provided.

☐ Go online to **www.pearsoned.co.uk/lawexpress** for more hands-on revision help and try out these resources:

  ☐ Try the **test your knowledge** quizzes and see if you can score full marks for each chapter.

  ☐ Attempt to answer the **sample questions** for each chapter within the time limit and check your answers against the guidelines provided.

  ☐ Listen to the **podcast** and then attempt the question it discusses.

  ☐ **'You be the marker'** and see if you can spot the strengths and weaknesses of the sample answers.

  ☐ Use the **flashcards** to test your recall of the legal principles of the key cases and statutes you've revised and the definitions of important terms.

Linking it all up

Essay or problem questions in criminology exams can be broken down into several fundamental issues:

✓ how crime can (and should be) defined and measured;

✓ the reasons why crime occurs; and

✓ what does (and should) be done to people who have committed crime, in terms of punishment

Taken together, these three key areas are all covered by the previous chapters in this guide.

Check where there are overlaps between subject areas. (You may want to review the 'revision note' boxes throughout this book.) Make a careful note of these as knowing how one topic may lead into another can increase your marks significantly. Here are some examples:

■ The overlap between the different definitions of crime in Chapter 1 and the discussion of different theories of crime in Chapters 5 – 9 – writers' ideas about what crime should be are often closely linked to their ideas about what causes crime.

■ The overlap between the biological positivism discussed in Chapter 6 and the psychological theories of crime discussed in Chapter 7, many of which were influenced by positivist values and beliefs.

■ The links between the sociological theories of crime discussed in Chapter 8 and the more contemporary theories in Chapter 9, which retained the earlier focus on societal causes of crime, while moving further away from the positivist influence of the earlier theories.

Knowing your theories, theorists and sources

Make sure you know how to use relevant theories and theorists and key sources of information to support your answers. Use the table below to focus your revision of the key examples in each topic. To review the details of these, refer back to the particular chapter.

Key example (theory, theorist, or source)	How to use	Related topics
Chapter 1 – What Is crime?		
Sutherland's 'moral norms' approach	To show how definitions of crime can reflect public ideas on morality	Differential association theory
Becker's 'labelling' approach	To understand how certain people have the power to define crime and label others as 'criminal'	Labelling theory
Marxist approaches	To understand the view that the powerful in society can define crime to suit their own interests and marginalise others	Marxist criminology
Chapter 2 – Measuring crime		
Police-recorded crime statistics	To understand how official crime statistics are constructed, and how there is a 'dark figure' of unreported crime	British Crime Survey
British Crime Survey crime statistics	To appreciate ways in which the 'dark figure' of unreported crime can be revealed	Police recorded crime statistics
Constructivist and radical approaches	To understand how crime statistics have limitations and may be politically constructed	Marxist criminology

▶

Key example (theory, theorist, or source)	How to use	Related topics
Chapter 3 – Who commits crime?		
The Offender Index	To gain an appreciation of how court statistics can be used to build up a picture of who offends	The Cambridge Study
The Cambridge Study	To understand that offenders can self-report crime for a variety of reasons at different times in their lives	The Offender Index
Chapter 4 – Crime and the media		
Content analysis of media crime reports	To understand how, and how accurately, the different facets of the media report crime	Positivist criminology
Bandura's studies on the criminogenic media	To understand the ways in which people can learn criminal behaviour from media sources such as film and television	Bandura's psychological social learning theory
'Moral panic' media theory	To evaluate the extent to which exaggerated news coverage of crime can have knock-on effects on criminal justice in action, such as harsher sentencing	Labelling theory
Chapter 5 – Classicist criminology		
Beccaria's 'social contract'	To understand the principles of classicist criminology, revolving around freedom of choice to offend	Just deserts/ retributivist theories of punishment
Matza and Hirschi's control theories	To understand what stops people from committing crime, and how they can drift into and out of offending	Cognitive psychological theories
Situational crime prevention theory	To understand the extent to which changes to physical environment can prevent or deter crime in practice	Chicago School environmental criminology

Key example (theory, theorist, or source)	How to use	Related topics
Chapter 6 – Biological positivist criminology		
Lombroso's 'primitive criminal' theory	To appreciate how traditional biological positivism saw criminality as deriving from physical or biological abnormalities, and to understand how these ideas opposed classicist ideas of crime as free will	Classicist criminology
Ferri's bio-environmental theory	To understand the ways in which biological positivism theories can be combined with environmental explanations for crime to create a more complete understanding of crime	Chicago School environmental criminology
The Gluecks' hybrid body type theory	To understand how biological explanations for crime can be combined with social and psychological factors for a fuller explanation of why crime occurs	Eysenck's biosocial psychological theory
Chapter 7 – Psychological explanations for crime		
Psychoanalytical theories	To analyse how various writers have attempted to explain crime through the existence of imbalances between the conscious and subconscious mind	Biological positivism
Learning theories	To understand the ways in which crime can be learned automatically through external factors	Differential association theory
Bandura's social learning theory	To appreciate how crime can be learned through the process of human thought and understanding	Bandura's studies on the criminogenic media
Eysenck's biosocial theory	To understand the ways in which crime can be understood by assessing the personality type of individual offenders	The Gluecks' hybrid body type positivist criminology

▶

Key example (theory, theorist, or source)	How to use	Related topics
Chapter 8 – Sociological explanations of crime		
Chicago School environmental criminology	To understand how crime can be explained by reference to a person's geographical environment and the levels of social control in that area	Ferri's bio-social positivist theory
Differential association theory	To gain knowledge of how crime involvement can be determined by how much a person associates with other offenders	Sutherland's 'moral norms' approach to defining crime; psychological learning theory
Strain and subcultural theories	To understand the argument that crime is caused by strain between social ambition and opportunity to achieve financial or status success	Chicago School environmental criminology
Labelling theory	To appreciate how crime could be caused by the reactions and labelling of behaviour which is seen as socially deviant	Labelling approach to crime definition; media moral panic theory
Chapter 9 – Contemporary criminology		
Marxist criminology	To understand the argument that crime is caused by the powerful in society's manipulation of criminal law and repression of the lower-class population	Marxist approaches to crime definition; constructivist and radical approaches to measuring crime
Left realism	To appreciate the standpoint that crime is caused by social divisions, but most offenders and victims come from a lower-class background – and to understand how these views differ from those held by Marxist criminology	Marxist criminology
Gender-based criminologies	To understand how supporters of a feminist or masculinity-based understanding of how crime occurs have argued that crime is best explained by the different social roles and experiences attributed to different genders	Labelling theory; psychological cognitive and learning theories

Key example (theory, theorist, or source)	How to use	Related topics
Chapter 10 – Theories of justice and penology		
Reductivist justifications	To understand how punishment can be justified in practice by preventing and reducing future crime, opposing retributivism	Retributivist justifications; classicist criminology
Retributivist/just deserts justifications	To understand how punishment can be justified in practice by punishing offenders on the basis that past criminal conduct deserves punishment proportionate to the crime committed, opposing reductivism	Reductivist justifications
Restorative justifications	To understand how punishment can be justified in practice by the offender making amends to the victim of the crime, therefore punishing past behaviour and preventing future offending	Reductivist justifications; retributivist justifications
Marxist and Foucauldian explanations	To gain a critical understanding of how the nature of punishment can be explained by the powerful in society maintaining and exploiting their authority, or by dispersing social control throughout society	Marxist criminology; Marxist approaches to crime definition
Cultural explanations	To gain a critical understanding of how the nature of punishment can be explained by the features of a society's culture, such as religion	Strain, subcultural and labelling theories of crime
Garland's adaptive theory of punishment	To gain a critical understanding of how the nature of punishment can be explained by combining the features of Marxist and cultural approaches, to show how governments hide their failings through excessive punishment	Marxist explanations for punishment; cultural explanations for punishment

■ Sample question

Below is an essay question that incorporates overlapping areas of criminology. See if you can answer this question drawing upon your knowledge of the whole subject area. Guidelines on answering this question are included at the end of this section.

ESSAY QUESTION

'Modern criminological and penological theory is mostly characterised by sociological ideas, but these ideas have struggled to impact upon current criminal justice policy, which focuses on individual responsibility for crime.' Critically discuss.

Answer guidelines

Approaching the question

This question asks you to contrast recent developments in academic criminological and penological thought with recent developments in criminal justice policy, focusing on the debate between individual and societal explanations for crime and punishment. It requires you to discuss the range of modern criminological and penological theories, but also their impact on criminal justice policy, so you would need to balance the two analytical aspects of the question in your answer.

Important points to include

- Introduction showing awareness of the range and diversity of modern criminological and penological theory.

- Discussion of the key principles of the range of modern criminological theories and the relative importance they give to social and individual causes, such as Marxism and its offshoots such as zemiology (clearly focused on social causes of crime) and right realism, psychological and crime prevention theories (clearly focused on individual responsibility for crime).

- Discussion of the key principles of the range of modern penological theories and the relative importance they give to social and individual explanations of and justifications for punishment, such as reductivism (focus on individual deterrence, but also society's protection from crime), retributivism (focus on individual responsibility for past crime); reparation (focus on individual responsibility, but also community reintegration after punishment); Marxist and Foucauldian explanations (clear focus on social explanations for punishment); cultural explanations (priority on social explanations, but recognition of individual effects of punishment too); and Garland's adaptive theory (focus on culture of control, with some individual elements).

■ Critical analysis of the relative effects of the criminological theories discussed on criminal justice policy in England and Wales in the recent past.

■ Critical analysis of the relative effects of the penological theories discussed on criminal justice policy in England and Wales in the recent past.

■ Conclusion summarising the relative importance of socially and individually based theory in recent criminological and penological theory, and in recent criminal justice policy.

✓ Make your answer stand out

■ When discussing hybrid theories such as left realism or Garland's adaptive theory of punishment, unpick the various influences on that theory carefully in terms of assessing the relative influences of social and individual explanations on that theory.

■ Quote directly from the academics who developed the key theories you discuss, showing detailed and direct knowledge of complex theories such as Garland's, rather than just quoting a textbook summary.

■ Acknowledge the influence of psychological theory on both criminology and criminal justice policy, as well as the various sociological influences.

Glossary of terms

The glossary is divided into two parts: key definitions and other useful terms. The key definitions can be found within the chapter in which they occur as well as in the glossary below. These definitions are the essential terms that you must know and understand in order to prepare for an exam. The additional list of terms provides further definitions of useful terms and phrases which will also help you answer examination and coursework questions effectively. These terms are highlighted in the text as they occur but the definition can only be found here.

Key definitions

Biological positivist criminology   A set of ideas which claims to explain why crime is committed by identifying certain biological characteristics of or inside a person's body, which are forcing that person to offend.

Classicist criminology   A set of ideas which argues that crime is the result of individuals' voluntary decisions to offend, having weighed up the advantages and disadvantages of committing crime rationally.

Contemporary criminology   A set of theoretical explanations for why crime occurs which have emerged in the past 50 years or so, and which seek to build on and improve previous explanations of crime by refining them or by combining elements from one or more previous theories together.

Crime Behaviour which is prohibited by the criminal law and which can be punished by the criminal justice system.

Crime statistics A range of ways of measuring crime which give information about how many offences there are in a particular place and over a particular period of time, trends in the number of particular criminal offences or in crime generally over time, how many people are the victims of crime and how often they are victimised, and/or how often crime occurs in a particular area or to a particular social group.

The 'dark figure' of crime Crime which is not reported to the police by the public, and which therefore cannot be included in police recorded crime statistics.

Explanatory theories of punishment A set of theoretical explanations for the nature of punishment in a particular time or place, and its past and future development, based on past and current evidence on the development of punishment in a particular time and place.

Justificatory theories of punishment A set of theoretical rationales and justifications for the nature of punishment, based on the perceived fairness and/or efficiency of a punishment system which conforms to the beliefs included as part of these theories.

Psychological criminology A set of theories which focus on the personality, learning processes, emotions, and other brain-related activities within an individual's mind as explanations for why crime is committed.

Sociological criminology A set of theoretical explanations for why crime occurs, which focus on conditions in society and geographical environment as the primary explanation for why individuals commit crime, rather than individual, biological or psychological factors within a particular individual.

■ Other useful terms

Biochemical criminology A type of biological positivist criminology which attempts to explain crime through differences in the internal biological and/or chemical characteristics of known offenders.

British Crime Survey

A national victimisation survey which gathers data from a representative sample of the British public about their experiences as victims of crime in the past.

Cognitive theories

Psychological theories which attempt to explain crime through the processes by which offenders think, solve problems and make choices about their lives.

Content analysis

A type of research which analyses the nature and extent of the reporting of crime by the media.

Control theory

A theory which attempts to explain criminal behaviour by examining the internal and external factors that discourage people from committing crime.

Cultural criminology

A theory which attempts to explain crime through a greater understanding of the excitement and escapism experienced by those who commit crime, and through the cultural resistance of certain groups to social and economic conditions in society.

Cultural penology

A set of theories which attempt to explain punishment with reference to the cultural conditions and circumstances in the society in which a particular set of punishment processes take place.

Delinquency opportunity theory

A theory of crime which explains offending through the formation of gangs to obtain either social status or financial wealth, with the formation of these gangs being dependent upon the available opportunities for delinquency in a particular social environment.

Deterrence

A reductivist theory which attempts to justify punishment by its ability to deter either offenders or others in society from committing crime in the future, through the direct or indirect experience of one's own or another's punishment.

Differential association

A theory which attempts to explain crime through the extent to which offenders associate and interact with other offenders.

Environmental criminology

A theory which attempts to explain crime through the geographical environment in which known offenders live and through the level of social disorganisation in particular inner-city areas.

Feminist criminologies   A set of theories which attempt to explain crime through exposing the social and economic discrimination experienced by women in society, and through the discrimination faced by female offenders in the criminal justice process.

Genetic criminology   A type of biological positivist criminology which attempts to explain crime through differences in the genetic profile of known offenders.

Incapacitation   A reductivist theory which attempts to justify punishment by physically removing a person's ability to commit crime in the future, either temporarily or permanently.

Labelling theory   A theory which attempts to explain crime through the labelling of certain types of behaviour as 'deviant' or 'criminal' by those who have enough social power to impose these labels, such as criminal justice agencies, the government and the media.

Learning theories   Psychological theories which attempt to explain crime through the processes by which people interact with, and learn criminal behaviour from, others around them.

Left realist criminology   A theory which attempts to explain crime through a mixture of social inequality and individual reactions to it, as well as through the consideration of crime victims' experiences.

Local victimisation surveys   Local-level crime victimisation surveys which seek to gather data from particular types of crime victim, living in particular geographical areas, thereby aiming to build up a more detailed picture of the nature and occurrence of particular types of crime.

Marxist criminology   A theory which attempts to explain crime through processes of economic inequality and oppression in capitalist society, and through the marginalisation, criminalisation, protest and masking of crimes committed by the powerful which results from these processes.

Marxist penology   A set of theories which attempt to explain punishment with reference to the economic conditions and inequalities in the society in which a particular set of punishment processes take place.

Masculinity criminologies

A set of theories which attempt to explain crime through the experiences of men in society, and the discrimination faced by certain social groups of men, inside and outside the criminal justice process.

Moral panic

The process by which certain types of crime are exaggerated and distorted by their coverage in the media, thereby leading to public unrest about these events and a harsher response to them by law and criminal justice.

Newsworthiness

The processes by which the media select particular crime-related events as being suitable for inclusion in their output.

Notifiable offences

Criminal offences which are included in police crime statistics.

The Offenders Index

Data produced by the government about who commits crime in England and Wales based on court statistics.

Psychoanalytical theories

Psychological theories which attempt to explain crime through imbalances in the conscious and subconscious mind of offenders.

Reductivism

A set of theories which attempt to justify punishment through the prevention of further offending in the future.

Rehabilitation

A reductivist theory which attempts to justify punishment by its ability to treat offenders in such a way that their offending behaviour will not recur in future.

Reparation

A set of theories which attempt to justify punishment through the idea of an offender making amends to their victim, or to the wider community, in some way.

Retributivism

A set of theories which attempt to justify punishment through the idea that punishment should be a deserved and proportionate reaction to offending which has already occurred.

Right realism

A theory which attempts to explain crime through a mixture of individual freedom of choice to commit crime, and behaviour which is either learned through upbringing or inherited in genetic terms.

Self-report study

A type of research into who commits crime which relies upon offenders disclosing the nature and extent of crime that they have committed in the past.

Social construct

The shaping, redefinition and manipulation of a concept (such as crime) through the processes by which it is interpreted and defined by individuals or groups in society.

Social control

A theory which attempts to explain punishment by the ways in which it is able to control, monitor and discipline behaviour in society which is seen as being threatening to the interests of the powerful.

Socially harmful acts

Behaviour which is viewed as being criminal due to its causing of harm to individuals within society or to society in general.

Strain theory

A theory which attempts to explain crime through a person's ambitions to succeed financially being blocked by the lack of legitimate opportunities to achieve financial success in society.

Situational crime prevention theory

A method of explaining and preventing crime which assumes that crime will be voluntarily committed if there is no obstacle to a person committing it, and therefore advocates reducing crime by removing physical opportunities to commit crime for potential offenders.

Subcultural theory

A theory of crime which explains offending through the formation of various forms of subcultural gangs which commit crime in order to obtain the social status denied to them by mainstream society.

Techniques of neutralisation

The process by which criminal or deviant behaviour is made to seem less serious and important by the words, actions and thoughts of those people who commit this type of behaviour.

Zemiology

A theory which attempts to explain crime through viewing it as one of a range of types of socially harmful behaviour.

Index